BOKO HARAM

DEADLY TERRORISM IN NIGERIA

By The Associated Press

Mango Media
Miami
in collaboration with
The Associated Press

   AP EDITIONS

AP Editions

Copyright © 2015 Associated Press. All rights reserved. This material may not be published, broadcast, rewritten or redistributed.

Published by Mango Media, Inc.
www.mangomedia.us

No part of this publication may be reproduced, distributed or transmitted in any form or by any means, without prior written permission.

This is a work of non-fiction adapted from articles and content by journalists of The Associated Press and published with permission.

Boko Haram *Deadly Terrorism in Nigeria*
ISBN: 978-1-63353-1536

Cover Photo:

This image taken from a video of Imam Abubakar Shekau cements his leadership in Boko Haram, January 10, 2012. (AP Photo)

Publisher's Note

AP Editions brings together stories and photographs by the professional journalists of The Associated Press.

These stories are presented in their original form and are intended to provide a snapshot of history as the moments occurred.

We hope you enjoy these selections from the front lines of newsgathering.

"It's not just the perpetrators who often murdered people in horrific ways who have not been held accountable, but also the political leaders and sometimes the religious leaders that foment violence, as well as the security forces who've used excessive force to respond to it."

- Corinne Dufka, senior West Africa researcher at Human Rights Watch

Table of Contents

Overview 1
Introduction 3
Early Violence 9
New Leader, More Killing 25
Goodluck Jonathan 51
Human Rights 75
Spilling Over Borders 97
Bring Back Our Girls 117
Joining the Islamic State Group 151

Overview

In early 2015, the Islamic State group accepted a pledge of allegiance by the Nigerian-grown Boko Haram extremists. The development raised concerns around the world that the violentAfrican group could extend its influence far beyond Nigeria and its bordering countries.

Boko Haram burst on the scene about a decade ago, attacking police stations and killing those who didn't adhere to a strict interpretation of Shariah Law. Its name translates as "Western education is sin." In 2011, it took credit for the bombing of United Nations headquarters in Abuja, Nigeria, that killed more than a dozen people.

The Associated Press has followed Boko Haram's path from its early raids to its horrific abduction in 2014 of 300 school girls. Through the camera lens and the written word, AP brings the story of this dangerous group to light.

Introduction

This file photo taken from video by Nigeria's Boko Haram terrorist network shows their leader Abubakar Shekau. Suspected Boko Haram militants attacked a village on the shore of Lake Chad early February 13, 2015, marking the first such violence against the neighbor contributing the most military might to the regional fight against the Nigeria-based terror group, May 12, 2014. (AP Photo/File)

Boko Haram Joins Islamic State
March 8, 2015
By Michelle Faul

Boko Haram's bid to forge an alliance with the Islamic State group in sub-Saharan Africa will provide only a propaganda boost for now, but in the long term it could internationalize a conflict restricted to Nigeria for nearly six years, analysts say.

The effort comes as both Islamic extremist groups have lost ground in recent weeks and as Nigeria's neighbors are forming a multinational army to confront Boko Haram.

By pledging allegiance to IS, Nigeria's home-grown militants have severed ties to al-Qaida, which is more powerful in the region, said Charlie Winter, a researcher at the London-based Quilliam Foundation.

Boko Haram has never been an affiliate of al-Qaida, but its militants fought alongside al-Qaida-linked groups during northern Mali's Islamic uprising two years ago, and some of its fighters have been trained in Somalia by al-

Shabab, another group with ties to al-Qaida, according to the group's propaganda.

Boko Haram's leader, Abubakar Shekau, reportedly pledged allegiance to IS leader Abu Bakr al-Baghdadi in an audio posted Saturday on Twitter. It could take three or four weeks for IS to formally respond, as has been the case with affiliates in Egypt, Yemen and Libya.

Leader of the Islamic State group, Abu Bakr al-Baghdadi, delivering a sermon at a mosque in Iraq during his first public appearance, July 5, 2014. (AP Photo/Militant video, File)

An alliance "would lend a more imposing quality to Islamic State with its expansionist model," Winter said. The move was symbolically "a striking development," but he doubted it would "change things on the ground in either Nigeria or Iraq and Syria."

But "over time this pledge of allegiance might lead to the internationalization" of a threat that until now has been mostly confined to a single region of Nigeria with occasional spillover into neighboring countries, warned J. Peter Pham, director of the Washington-based Atlantic Council's Africa Center.

Boko Haram was little known until its April 2014 abduction of nearly 300 Nigerian schoolgirls from a school in the remote town of Chibok drew international outrage. At the time, al-Baghdadi praised the Nigerian insurgents and said the mass kidnapping was justification for the IS abduction of Yazidi women and girls in northern Iraq.

A partnership with IS could also be a recruiting tool. Fighters from IS franchises in North Africa who find it harder to migrate to the Middle East may choose to move to a Boko Haram emirate instead, Pham said.

The international support pouring into anti-Boko Haram forces from the United States, France, the United Kingdom and others "may render the Nigerian militants' fight all the more attractive to these foreign jihadists," Pham said.

The core of Boko Haram's estimated 4,000 to 6,000 militants is from the Kanuri tribe, which spreads across colonial-era borders in a region where people show stronger allegiance to tribes than states.

In August, Boko Haram declared it was reviving an ancient Islamic caliphate in northeastern Nigeria that spilled over those borders, in a move copying the Islamic State group. But Boko Haram's brutality, including beheadings and enslavement, predates and in some cases arguably exceeds that of IS, according to Pham.

Pham expects Boko Haram to engage in even more gruesome tactics if it wins the support of IS.

"The upcoming Nigerian elections and potential postelection upheaval provide too rich of a target environment for the jihadists to pass up," Pham said.

Nigerian President Goodluck Jonathan is running for re-election in a March 28 ballot that analysts say is too close to call and that Boko Haram has threatened to disrupt, calling democracy a corrupt Western concept.

In some ways, Pham said, an alliance could work against Boko Haram. Becoming another IS province could mean losing its ethnic appeal among Kanuris and its appeal among ordinary Nigerians for whom denunciations of corruption involving Nigeria's political elites resonate.

Joining IS would also require major strategy changes by Boko Haram that could cause friction, Winter said, explaining that Boko Haram would have to adopt the IS model of an Islamist utopia by providing health care and other social services taken on by IS in its state-building efforts.

Boko Haram has seized a large swath of northeastern Nigeria in the past eight months — an area perhaps as large as Belgium. But it has largely brutalized people who remain behind, enforcing its version of strict Islamic law by carrying out public whippings and severing of limbs of alleged transgressors.

The possibility of an IS-Boko Haram alliance has been on the table for months, and Saturday's pledge probably followed weeks of negotiations about how each group can benefit, Winter said.

Nigerian President Goodluck Jonathan gestures, during an election campaign rally in Lagos, Nigeria. The six-week delay in Nigeria's presidential election has raised red flags both in the international community and among local opposition political groups, with many concerned about the independence of the country's electoral commission and whether the military hierarchy had too much say in the matter. President Goodluck Jonathan and his chief rival, former military dictator Muhammadu Buhari, are facing off in what is probably the tightest presidential contest in the history of Nigeria, Africa's most populous nation, January 8, 2015. (AP Photo/Sunday Alamba, File)

Boko Haram may expect financial support from IS, which is still probably the wealthiest extremist group in the world despite recent drops in the price of oil that is the mainstay of the IS economy, Winter said.

More difficult would be IS support in training and manpower, given the geographical challenges, he said.

An alliance provides both groups with an immediate propaganda boost. Boko Haram stands to receive a new presence in social media, thanks to IS propagandists whose slick videos could replace Boko Haram's often incoherent and muddled messages.

And if the IS network of supporters start spreading Boko Haram propaganda, that will "project its influence and exaggerate its menace," Winter said.

Professor Abubakar Mustapha said just the idea of Boko Haram symbolically joining forces with IS enough to frighten some Nigerians.

"It will outrage and scare people," said the professor of Islamic Studies at Bayero University Kano, in northern Nigeria.

1

Early Violence

A girl walks past a wall with graffiti about the al-Qaida network, in a Muslim area of the northern city of Kano, Nigeria. A bloody failed uprising to create a Taliban-style state in Africa's most populous nation appears an isolated rebellion of rich boys, launched by a small, Afghanistan-inspired cadre of university students using family wealth, not al-Qaida funding, April 18, 2003. (AP Photo/Schalk van Zuydam)

Nigerian Taliban
January 14, 2004
By Oloche Samual and John Murray

A bloody uprising aimed at creating a Taliban-style state in Africa's most populous nation appears to have been a rebellion by students who got money from family, not al-Qaida, officials and captive fighters told The Associated Press.

Security forces of Nigeria and neighboring Niger quashed the Afghan-inspired students' offensive, which was led by an Islamic cleric. Even with the campaign defeated, and dozens of rebels dead, in jail or in hiding, the students are unrepentant.

"Policeman are agents who protect the ungodly," 21-year-old student Mohammed told AP, sitting in police custody, his round face wrinkled in disgust. "We have a duty to follow Allah's law, and show people the way."

Mohammed, son of two former senior officials from a prominent family in the north, spoke on condition his last name not be used.

The two-week uprising, routed by Jan. 3, ended with at least two policemen and 16 others dead, mostly students - including 10 killed by Nigerian villagers and Niger security forces as the men tried to fight their way across the border after being defeated by Nigeria's army and police.

Residents told AP they believe the death toll in the northern state of Yobe, scene of the uprising, was higher - around 50, with students making up most of the dead. At least 10,000 civilians in several towns fled the fighting, Yobe state emergency officials said.

At its height, students stripped three police stations of arms and ammunition and set the stations and other government buildings afire. Students used the looted AK-47s to battle police.

A police officer looks through his riot helmet in the northern city of Kano, Nigeria, May 26, 2003. (AP Photo/Schalk van Zuydam)

The uprising - which appalled most Muslims in northern Nigeria - came without warning, and virtually without precedent. Except for an Islamic uprising in northern Nigeria in the 1980s, Nigeria and West Africa as a whole have seen none of the kind of armed Islamic movements that have plagued other regions.

In West Africa, "there's a brewing religious intolerance in some places, but it's mostly fueled by political leaders. Most people left to their own devices aren't becoming fundamentalists," said Ross Herbert at the South African Institute of International Affairs in Johannesburg.

"In West Africa, people have too many other problems to worry about fomenting global revolution," he said.

Modeled on the Taliban, the movement emerged during four years of rising Muslim-Christian tensions inside Nigeria.

Religious violence - mostly sudden clashes between Muslim and Christian mobs - has killed thousands in Nigeria since 1999. In that year, Yobe and 11 other predominantly Islamic northern states began introducing Islamic law, or Shariah.

Eighteen year-old Hajara Ibrahim at the court waiting room while a police officer stands guard in Dass, 25 miles south of the state capital of Bauchi, Nigeria. Ibrahim who is seven months pregnant was sentenced to death by stoning by a lower Sharia court in Lere for committing adultery, but she is appealing at the Sharia higher court in Dass, October 27, 2004. (AP Photo/George Osodi)

The students were followers of a Nigerian Islamic cleric known as Abu Umar, or Mullah Umar, students and Nigerian security agencies told AP.

Little is known about Umar except that he, like all his followers, is under age 30. He drew his flock largely from northern Islamic states, but also from the majority Christian southern states of Oyo, Osun and Lagos.

The students included children of top northern government officials, police said. The young men called themselves Al Sunna wal Jamma, Arabic loosely translated as Followers of the Prophet's Teaching.

Leaving prosperous homes and university study, the students settled with Mullah Umar in a tent city on the banks of the Yobe River at the town of Kanamma.

At least 200 students lived there - roughly the same number as is believed to have taken part in the uprising, said Yobe state spokesman Ibrahim Jirgi. Security agencies say the group may secretly have had as many as 1,000 members, spread out in cells.

Authorities have found no links to Afghanistan's deposed Taliban regime, al-Qaida or other outside groups - but haven't ruled them out - a top security official said, speaking on condition of anonymity.

Investigators do have one key question, the official said: Where, and how, did university students learn how to handle arms?

"We certainly know they received some weapons training, because they're not taught sharp-shooting in school," he said. "What we now want to know is who gave them the military training - are they Nigerians, or foreigners?"

Mohammed said a friend introduced him to Mullah Umar, when Mohammed was an economics student at Bayero University in the northern city of Kano.

"Umar saw my interest in the Koran and the Islamic way of life," the jailed student said. "So he showed me portions of the Koran which says we should consider those who don't follow Allah's law as followers of Satan."

The students' simple adopted lifestyle required little money, and what they needed came from their families. Sons of well-off families could "collect money from their parents under any pretext," Mohammed said.

Mohammed spoke to AP at police headquarters in Maiduguri, capital of northeastern Borno state. Troops captured him in a group of students Jan. 1, in an ambush outside the city.

Umar eluded arrest, and is being sought by authorities.

Under Mullah Umar, the group for two years limited itself to political activity - handing out leaflets critical of officials they saw as lax on Islamic law, for example.

Then, the sect began clashing with residents over fishing rights around their Yobe River camp.

Increasingly militant, students took over a primary school in Kanamma, hoisting a flag that labeled it "Afghanistan."

Yobe state Gov. Abba Ibrahim said he was trying to persuade the students to disband when they launched their attacks.

The offensive failed, not only because security troops moved in, but because the rich students failed to connect with the area's Muslims - 80 percent of whom live on less than $1 a day.

"They put Islam upside down," said Ibrahim Tijjani, a Maiduguri-based Muslim cleric. "Violence is only justifiable in Islam when one's religion, life, family or property is attacked - none of which happened in this case."

Attacking the Police
July 28, 2009
By Bashir Adigun

Islamist militants seeking to impose a Taliban-style regime in northern Nigeria launched attacks Monday (July 27) on police in three towns, expanding a two-day campaign of violence that has killed at least 55 people, police and witnesses said.

Trouble began Sunday when militants attacked a police station in the northern city of Bauchi, leaving dozens dead in gunbattles with police. On Monday, militants launched a wave of attacks in three more states, targeting the towns of Maiduguri, Damaturu, and Wudil in the predominantly Muslim North, police and residents said.

National police chief Ogbonnaya Onovo put the overall toll at 55 dead at least 50 militants and five police officers.

A journalist for the local Compass newspaper in Maiduguri, Olugbenga Akinbule, said he saw the bodies of about 100 Islamist militants shot in gunbattles with police in the town, where some of the worst violence occurred. Authorities did not confirm that toll.

Bodies lie in the street in Maiduguri in front of police headquarters following clashes between Islamic militants and police, July 27, 2009. (AP Photo/Gbenga Akinbule)

Nigeria has been sporadically wracked by sectarian clashes since 12 of the country's 36 states began adopting Islamic law, or Shariah, in the north in 1999.

The radical sect known as Al-Sunna wal Jamma, or "Followers of Mohammed's Teachings" in Arabic, comprises mainly young Nigerians who want to create a Taliban-style state based on a strict interpretation of Shariah Law and the Quran. The group first came to prominence with a wave of similar assaults on New Year's Eve 2003. More attacks followed in late 2004, but little has been heard about the sect since.

Residents in the North also refer to the Islamists as "Boko Haram," which means "Western education is sin" in the local Hausa dialect. Onovo referred to the militants as Taliban, though the group has no known links to Taliban fighters in Afghanistan.

A local newspaper, Daily Trust, quoted the leader of the sect, Ustaz Mohammed Yusuf, as saying his followers are ready to die to ensure the institution of a strict Islamic society.

"Democracy and (the) current system of education must be changed, otherwise this war that is yet to start would continue for long," he said.

Onovo vowed that police would arrest the group's leaders.

"This a fanatical organization that is anti-government, anti-people. We don't know what their aims are yet; we are out to identify and arrest their leaders and also destroy their enclaves, wherever they are," Onovo said.

In Damaturu, capital of Yobe state, militants bombed a police station, said national police spokesman Emmanuel Ojukwu.

In Kano state's Wudil district, militants attacked another police station, according to local police spokesman Baba Muhammad. He said three militants were killed and two police officers were wounded in a shootout, and 34 militants were arrested.

In Maiduguri, the capital of Borno state, militants battled police for hours. Onovo said he had sent "reinforcements to our men in Maiduguri to be able to cope with the situation." Akinbule said militants attacked a police headquarters, burned 10 houses inside the police compound, and freed prisoners from a state prison.

Nnamdi K. Obasi, a Nigerian analyst with the International Crisis Group, said trouble has been brewing for a while.

He said police in Maiduguri stopped some motorcycle-riding members of a funeral procession carrying the body of a sect member two months ago because they were not wearing helmets. A fracas ensued and police shot and killed 14 members of the group, prompting Yusuf to vow retaliation, Obasi said.

Police have been carrying out operations against the group. Last week in Biu, about 200 kilometers (125 miles) south of Maiduguri, they raided a militant compound and found homemade bombshells, explosive material, knives, machetes and guns, and arrested nine militants.

On Saturday, police in Maiduguri raided another house being used by the militants after a homemade bomb exploded there accidentally, killing one militant and injuring another, according to Onovo, who said police "recovered many bags of explosives and different types of dangerous weapons" from the house.

Obasi said the dead militant was a senior leader of the sect who group members believe state security forces assassinated. "Word went around their network that the police were carrying out pre-emptive searches, and this has led to the attacks since Sunday," Obasi said by telephone from Kearney, Nebraska.

More than 10,000 Nigerians have died in sectarian violence since civilian leaders took over from a former military junta in 1999, though in recent years such violence has eased.

Nigerian troops patrol in Maiduguri, August 1, 2009. AP Photo/Sunday Alamba)

Nigeria's 140 million people are nearly evenly divided between Christians, who predominate in the south, and primarily northern-based Muslims. Shariah was implemented in a dozen northern states after the country returned to civilian rule in 1999 following years of oppressive military regimes.

Obasi said, however, that Shariah was never strictly imposed, and politicians had used the promise to do so to consolidate their hold on power and attract funding from the Middle East.

The Islamist sect has been able to expand quietly since 2004, fueled by deepening poverty and lack of development.

"You find Islamic leaders coming forward to say, 'We've never gained anything from Western models of governance or education, and unless we go back to the society prescribed by the Quran, nothing will get better,'" Obasi said.

Nigerian Troops Attack Boko Haram Militants
July 28, 2009
By Njadvara Musa

Army troops traded fire with Islamic militants Tuesday (July 28) and deployed armored vehicles to surround the suspected hideout of a radical

Muslim leader accused of orchestrating three days of violence in Africa's most populous nation.

A tense calm returned to several towns elsewhere in northern Nigeria after authorities imposed curfews and poured security forces onto the streets to quell a wave of militant attacks against police, which have killed dozens of people since Sunday.

Appealing for calm, President Umaru Yar'Adua told reporters: "This situation is being brought under control."

Nigerian President Umaru Yar'Adua, September 27, 2007. (AP photo/David Karp)

Sporadic gunfire was reported through the day in Maiduguri, capital of Borno state, where some of the worst violence occurred Monday. Police exchanged intermittent fire with militants as they tried to raid their camps in the city, according to local journalist Olugbenga Akinbule. He said more than 3,000 people had been displaced in the city.

Later in the day, the army sent armored vehicles to Maiduguri and deployed them in a residential district that is believed to be a stronghold of the sect. Officers said they believed militant leader Ustaz Mohammed Yusuf was holed up in a house in the district.

As army vehicles approached and opened fire, sect members fired back, soldiers said. An Associated Press reporter in the area saw smoke billowing above homes.

Army Maj. Gen. Saleh Maina said troops were hunting for sect members in homes and a mosque and near the Maiduguri railway station. He said the operation was being carried out "to prevent further loss of lives and property."

Troops and police had begun blocking off the area Monday, sealing streets and ordering residents to leave for their own safety. Elsewhere in the city, the bodies of dozens of dead militants lay on roadsides.

National police chief Ogbonnaya Onovo said Monday at least 55 people have died in the violence since it began Sunday, including 50 militants and five police officers. His spokesman Emmanuel Ojukwu said Tuesday authorities were still adding up the number of dead and arrested, and declined to give total figures.

A Nigerian trooper walks past burned out motorbikes in Maiduguri, August 1, 2009. (AP photo/Sunday Alamba)

Nigeria's 140 million people are nearly evenly divided between Christians, who predominate in the south, and primarily northern-based Muslims. Shariah was implemented in 12 northern states after Nigeria returned to civilian rule in 1999 following years of oppressive military regimes. More than 10,000 Nigerians have died in sectarian violence since then.

The radical sect behind the latest violence is known by several different names, including Al-Sunna wal Jamma, or "Followers of Mohammed's Teachings" in Arabic, and "Boko Haram," which means "Western education is sin" in the local Hausa dialect. Onovo referred to the militants as Taliban, although the group has no known affiliation with Taliban fighters in Afghanistan.

The group, which wants to see traditional government replaced by a Taliban-style state based on a strict interpretation of Shariah law and the Quran, first gained notoriety with a similar wave of assaults on New Year's Eve 2003. More attacks followed in late 2004.

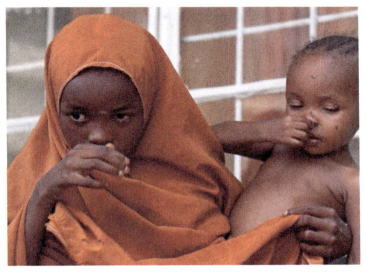

Children of suspected Islamist sect members seen at a police station where they have been kept for their safety during violence in in Maiduguri. Nigerian authorities ignored dozens of warnings about a violent Islamist sect until it attacked police stations and government buildings last week in a bloodbath that killed more than 700 people, August 2, 2009. (AP photo/Sunday Alamba)

Analysts say trouble has brewed for months, as police began raiding militant hideouts and finding explosives and arms.

Yar'Adua said the Islamic militants had been "preparing arms, learning how to make explosives and bombs to disturb our peace and force their ideas on the rest of Nigerians."

"Luckily, our security forces have been tracking them for years and I believe that the operation we have launched now will be an operation that will contain them once and for all," he said, referring to Maiduguri.

"What we have now is the situation in Borno state where the leader of the so-called Taliban group is resident, where most of them have migrated from all over the northern states to prepare, and declare a holy war," Yar'Adua said.

The president also said security forces would continue "security surveillance all over the northern states to fish out any remnants of these elements and deal with them."

The latest violence began Sunday in the northern city of Bauchi and spread the next day to three other predominantly Muslim northern states.

Mohammed Maigari Khanna, a spokesman for the governor of Bauchi state, said security forces Tuesday were searching for militants who had tried to flee and had arrested some of them. He said a dusk-to-dawn curfew had been imposed and security agents had blanketed the area.

In Kano state's Wudil district, where militants on Monday attacked a police station, 17 people were arrested overnight, bringing the total detained there to 53, according to Kano police spokesman Baba Mohammed. He said Kano was calm and police reinforcements had arrived to back up local security forces.

Boko Haram Leader Killed in Police Custody
July 30, 2009
By Njadvara Musa and Michelle Faul

Lecturers tore up their degrees and abandoned universities to join him. Others bankrupted themselves, selling cars and other valuables to honor his call to give up Western trappings for the sake of Islam.

Thousands made such sacrifices for Mohammed Yusuf, leader of a group sometimes called the Nigerian Taliban. The 39-year-old was shot and killed Thursday (July 30) in police custody after being found in a goat pen at the home of his in-laws.

Yusuf had escaped with some 300 followers as troops shelled his compound in the northern city of Maiduguri on Wednesday, killing some 100 members of the sect.

Yusuf's death could provoke more violence. Though his followers in the Boko Haram sect may be in disarray some lieutenants fled and others were arrested the decades-long grievances that caused followers to flock to his cause remain.

The sect, with its anti-Western agenda, had been gathering disciples for years in Nigeria, a major oil producer and Africa's most populous nation.

Yusuf, a Western-educated member of the country's elite, encouraged his followers to rid themselves of all material wealth while he was chauffeured around in a Mercedes all-terrain vehicle and amassed dozens of vehicles at his compound.

Police stand alongside bodies of dead Islamic militants, in the street in front of police headquarters in Maidugiri. Army troops traded fire with Islamic militants and deployed armored vehicles to surround the suspected hideout of Mohammed Yusuf accused of orchestrating three days of violence, July 29, 2009. (AP photo/Gbenga Akingbule)

A university graduate who spoke excellent English, said he has discounted Darwinism, claimed the world cannot be round because the Koran does not say that and credited Allah with creating rain.

"We believe (rain) is a creation of God rather than an evaporation caused by the sun that condenses and becomes rain," he said in a BBC interview.

Militants with Boko Haram which in the local language means "Western education is sacrilege" attacked police stations, churches and government buildings in a wave of violence that began Sunday in Borno and quickly spread to three other northern states. The group is seeking the imposition of strict Islamic Shariah law in Nigeria, a multi-religious country.

The fighting was the first by the group since December 2007. Nigeria's military thought it annihilated the sect back then after it attacked police outposts in two northern states. But apparently it had just gone underground to prepare for something catastrophic.

Nnamdi K. Obasi, a Nigerian analyst with the International Crisis Group, said some members of the group have fought alongside the Taliban in Afghanistan and staunch supporters travel to Iraq and Sudan for inspiration. But their favored destination is Iran, which is considered almost a pilgrimage, he said.

A suspected Islamist sect member captured by Nigerian troops as he lies next to a tree in Maiduguri, August 1, 2009. (AP photo/Sunday Alamba)

Most sect members are young, disgruntled people. Although most are poor and unemployed, some come from highly educated and elite families. They are angry that the introduction of moderate Shariah law in 12 northern states 10 years ago has not halted the corruption that keeps most Nigerians impoverished while a coterie of millionaires prosper from the country's prodigious oil wealth.

"Those who were excited about the possibility of Sharia have been disappointed. Corruption ... did not stop when it came in," says Junaid Mohammed, a former member of Nigeria's parliament.

In its strictest application, Shariah dictates a kind of social welfare system with compassionate treatment for poorer members of society.

The sect abhors everything Western, including science, and blames British colonization and Western values for destroying their culture.

They would return to the "purity" of rule by a Muslim caliphate, topple Nigeria's government and impose strict Shariah law throughout this nation of

140 million people who speak more than 200 languages and are roughly divided between northern Muslims and Christian southerners.

A man walks past a burned out car and building in Maiduguri. Banks and markets reopened in this northern Nigerian city after five days of fierce fighting between police and a radical Islamist sect that left at least 300 people dead, August 1, 2009. (AP photo/Sunday Alamba)

That is unlikely given the group's small numbers, its bases only in northern Nigeria, the nation's largely secular leanings and the sect's primitive armory of homemade hunting rifles, firebombs, bows and arrows, scimitars and machetes.

But they can create mayhem.

For three days this week they tied down thousands of troops and police until security forces shelled their headquarters Wednesday night and then stormed their mosque.

President Yar'Adua said he ordered attacks this week after Yusuf called followers from other states to his headquarters, preparing to unleash jihad, "the holy war."

No one knows precisely how many followers Yusuf has, but they are estimated in the thousands. Obasi said Yusuf seemed to have several hundred core followers in the capitals of 12 northern states and a few thousand supporters in each urban center. The sect is strongest in the northeast states of Borno, Bauchi and Yobe.

Like Palestinian militants to whom they are not known to have ties Yusuf's followers believe the greatest honor is to die fighting for their cause, Obasi said.

Yusuf won some unlikely converts. Like Musa Kabir, a lecturer at Bauchi's Abubakar Tafawa Balewa University who six months ago publicly shredded his master's degree in engineering.

"I now understand that it is not right for me to hold anything that portrays Western education or culture," he declared.

In their zeal to give monetary support to their cause and rid themselves of Western trappings, people have sold their homes and vehicles.

"The ideology of the group says get rid of material possessions, even a wristwatch; that these Western things have been created to divert you from your course of worshipping Allah," Obasi explains.

Some accuse the group of using doctored palm dates and wooden chewing sticks to charm people into their circle.

"Some people were forcefully coerced to join after they ate those dates," says Ibrahim Gumai, a retired civil servant and small businessman who used to be close to sect leaders.

Obasi has not heard about the dates, but says "there is talk about the use of magical methods, casting spells on people ..."

New Leader, More Killing

Unidentified women react to the sight of dead bodies in Dogo Nahwa, Nigeria. More than 200 people, most of them Christians, were slaughtered on February 28 in central Nigeria, according to residents, aid groups and journalists, March 8, 2010. (AP Photos/Jon Gambrell)

Cycles of Violence
January 20, 2010
By Jon Gambrell

Charred bodies with scorched hands reaching skyward lay in the streets and a mosque with blackened minarets smoldered Wednesday (January 20) after several days of fighting between Christians and Muslims killed more than 200 people.

Sectarian violence in this central region of Nigeria has left thousands dead over the past decade, and the latest outbreak that began Sunday came despite the government's efforts to quell religious extremism in the West African country.

Jos was mostly calm Wednesday, though many terrified civilians kept indoors while soldiers patrolled the streets. The city is situated in Nigeria's "middle belt," where dozens of ethnic groups mingle in a band of fertile and hotly contested land separating the Muslim north from the predominantly Christian south.

There are conflicting accounts about what unleashed the bloodshed. According to the state police commissioner, skirmishes began after Muslim youths set a Christian church ablaze, but Muslim leaders denied that. Other community leaders say it began with an argument over the rebuilding of a Muslim home in a predominantly Christian neighborhood that had been destroyed in November 2008.

Nigerian troops provide security in Jos, Nigeria. Charred bodies lay in the streets and mosques with blackened smoldering minarets are seen in the area after several days of fighting between Christians and Muslims, with more than 200 people thought to be dead, January 20, 2010. (AP Photo/Sunday Alamba)

Corinne Dufka, senior West Africa researcher at Human Rights Watch, said what caused the latest spark was beside the point. The deeper problem, she said, is the government's failure to address underlying conflict in the region.

After similar bouts of violence in the past, Nigerian authorities have "come up with analysis, but they don't respond properly with concrete measures and policies," Dufka said. "Tensions seethe, and months or years later you have another outbreak."

More than 13,500 Nigerians have died in sectarian violence in the last decade, and at least 2,500 people had been killed in Plateau state alone since 2001, according to Human Rights Watch. Dufka said no one has been held accountable, leading to a climate of impunity.

A rescue worker looks on as people walk past a burnt body in Jos, January 20, 2010. (AP Photo/Sunday Alamba)

"It's not just the perpetrators who often murdered people in horrific ways who have not been held accountable, but also the political leaders and sometimes the religious leaders that foment violence, as well as the security forces who've used excessive force to respond to it."

In Jos, witnesses said rioters armed with knives, homemade firearms and stones had attacked passers-by and fought with security forces, leaving bodies in the street and stacked in mosques after fighting began Sunday.

Authorities imposed a 24-hour curfew, but on Wednesday people could be seen walking around the center of the city. When an army convoy passed, they stopped and raised their hands above their heads to show they were not a threat.

"We want the government to come and help us," said Abdullahi Ushman, who said he had seen rioters attacking people with firearms and bows and arrows.

Plateau State governor Jonah Jang said the violence was not provoked by a lack of opportunity in this rural farming community. He claimed many of the attackers were from Muslim-dominant northern Nigeria and from the nearby, predominantly Muslim nations of Niger and Chad.

"There are people masterminding this for their own selfish reasons," said Jang, who is Christian.

The Minister of Police Affairs, Ibrahim Yakubu Lame, issued a statement Tuesday blaming the violence on "some highly placed individuals in the society who were exploiting the ignorance and poverty of the people to cause mayhem in the name of religion."

The chief of Army staff, Lt. Gen. Abdulrahman Danbazau, confirmed accounts that some residents had been dragged out of their homes and shot by men dressed in what appeared to be army uniforms. He said five of the suspects arrested were dressed in khaki army-style uniforms and claimed to be police officers, though only one of the five men could provide police identification.

A local market that was destroyed in violence in Jos, January 20, 2010. (AP Photo/Sunday Alamba)

Jos is not alone in being shaken by religious violence. In July, an extremist group known as Boko Haram translated as "Western education is sacrilege" attacked police stations and other government buildings, starting days of violence that left more than 700 people dead in northern Nigeria. Another wave of violence started by infighting in another Islamic extremist group left at least 38 people dead in December.

Still, nearly all violence caused by extremist sects comes from intensely local politics or grievances not any call for holy war against the West.

The government has sought to distance itself from any al-Qaida links after a 23-year-old Nigerian was accused of trying to blow up a U.S.-bound flight on Christmas Day. Nigerian officials have said that Umar Farouk Abdulmutallab was influenced far beyond the nation's borders while studying in London and in Yemen.

Nnamdi Obasi, a Nigeria-based senior analyst for the International Crisis Group, said the government's response to previous cycles of violence in Jos has been to deploy soldiers without resolving the underlying tensions.

"There is poverty and desperation. So you very easily have mobs of young people ready to take out frustrations on other groups, especially when they can identify them as an opposing group, be it Muslim or Christian," Obasi said.

Extrajudicial Killings
March 1, 2010
By Nujadvara Musa

Nigerian police detained 17 officers for questioning after an international news channel aired a video showing uniformed men executing people in a town where religious rioting occurred, a spokesman said Monday (March 1).

Police spokesman Yemi Ajyai said agents of the Nigerian police's Special Forces Squad detained the officers over the weekend and took them to Abuja, the capital, for questioning. Ajyai said investigators suspect the officers took part in extrajudicial killings after fighting between police and Muslim militants left 700 people dead in northern Nigeria last year.

Ajyai said a video aired on news channel Al-Jazeera sparked the arrests. That footage showed what appeared to be a mixed police and army unit conducting door-to-door searches. It later showed two uniformed men forcing groups of young men to lie face-down at the side of a busy road. The uniformed men then fired into the men's backs. Their hands were tied behind their backs.

The video showed two others on crutches forced to lie down by the corpses and be shot, with the news channel describing an officer shouting: "Shoot him in the chest, not the head. I want his hat."

The footage could not be authenticated by The Associated Press.

The fighting began after militants from Boko Haram attacked a police station in Bauchi state in late July. Violence quickly spread to three other states before Nigerian forces retaliated, storming the group's Maiduguri compound.

Men detained by police, in the wake of religious violence in Jos, Nigeria, sit in a police waiting room. Witnesses say soldiers opened fire on angry youths who surrounded a cattle truck in Jos, March 10, 2010. (AP Photos/Jon Gambrell)

Nigerian police and army officials denied committing extrajudicial killings while responding to the rioting. However, human rights groups say such killings are common across the West African nation. Authorities have been accused of killing Boko Haram leader Mohammed Yusuf while he was in custody. Police officials say he was killed while trying to escape, but army officials said he was alive when he was arrested. On Feb. 9, when the video was shown, Al-Jazeera also aired footage that showed a dead man who closely resembled Yusuf, with his hands cuffed behind his back.

At the time, Borno state Police Commissioner Ibrahim Abdu described the video as false and "a deliberate attempt of the surviving sect members to cause confusion and threats." On Monday, Abdu declined to discuss why the men were detained.

"I cannot deny the arrests of some of my officers and men," Abdu said.

New Boko Haram Leader
July 1, 2010
By Jon Gambrell

A leader of a radical Muslim sect that started a rampage that left 700 people dead in Nigeria allegedly has issued a videotaped threat calling for new violence as the one-year anniversary of their attack nears.

Imam Abubakar Shekau, a sect deputy whom police claimed to have killed during the July 2009 violence, told a Nigerian journalist that he had taken over as leader of the Boko Haram sect. Shekau told the reporter that he suffered a gunshot wound to the thigh during the fighting, but had been rescued by "fellow believers and protected by Allah."

This image taken from a video of Imam Abubakar Shekau cements his leadership in Boko Haram, January 10, 2012. (AP Photo)

"I have the intention to retaliate," Shekau said in the local Hausa language.

The Associated Press could not immediately verify the authenticity of the recording seen by Nigeria's Daily Trust newspaper Thursday. Borno state police commander Ibrahim Abdu dismissed the videotape, but said security officials would take precautions as the anniversary of last year's violence draws near.

"Our officers and men are not taking chances," Abdu said.

He added: "Different security measures had already been put in, so that there is no breach of peace in any part of the state."

The newspaper said a reporter got the 25-minute interview with Shekau on April 19 after being blindfolded and driven to a hideout near Maiduguri, the site of much of the violence last year. The interview took place with Shekau seated before a stack of religious books and near a Kalashnikov rifle.

Asked where the sect obtains weapons, Shekau answered: "We get them from where we get them. God said we should get them, the holy prophet said we should get them."

Boko Haram has campaigned for the implementation of strict Shariah law. Nigeria, a nation of 150 million people, is divided between the Christian-dominated south and the Muslim-held north. A dozen states across Nigeria's north already have Shariah law in place, though the area remains under the control of secular state governments.

Boko Haram sect members rioted and attacked police stations and private homes a year ago this month, sparking a violent police crackdown. Authorities have been accused of killing Boko Haram leader Mohammed Yusuf while he was in custody. Police officials said he was killed while trying to escape, but army officials said he was alive when he was arrested.

The group largely went underground after Yusuf's death. In early March, police arrested 17 officers suspected of taking part in filmed executions that later aired on international news channel Al-Jazeera.

In recent months, rumors about the group rearming spread throughout northern Nigeria. Violence between Christians and Muslims in central Nigeria has left hundreds dead since the start of the year. Those deaths sparked calls from an al-Qaida-affiliated website for a Muslim uprising against Christians.

Abubakar Ibn Umar Garbai El-Kanemi, a traditional leader in Borno state, told journalists Wednesday that he also had information that Boko Haram followers planned an uprising. He asked locals to report any suspicious activity to police.

"We had reliable information that some of the sect's members are planning to infiltrate some of the communities and mosques they had abandoned during last year's sectarian crises," he said.

Prison Break
September 8, 2010
By Jon Gambrell and Shehu Saulawa

A radical Muslim sect used assault rifles to launch a coordinated sunset raid on a prison in northern Nigeria, freeing more than 100 followers and raising new fears about violence in the oil-rich nation just months before elections.

The attack Tuesday (September 7) night by the Boko Haram sect left the prison in ruins and showed the group had access to the sophisticated weapons it needed to overpower prison guards. Now the group seeking to impose strict Islamic law on Nigeria may want to take on the government directly, potentially bring a new wave of violence to Africa's most populous nation.

Soldiers secure the area outside a prison in Bauchi, Nigeria, after Boko Haram armed with assault rifles launched an attack at sunset on the prison to free more than 100 inmates who are followers of the sect. The highly organized and coordinated assault left the prison in ruins and has raised new fears of renewed violence in the oil-rich nation just months before scheduled elections, and shows they have access to sophisticated weaponry, September 9, 2010. (AP Photo/Sunday Alamba)

The Nigerian government is "standing flat-footed. They're on the defensive," said Mark Schroeder, the director of sub-Saharan Africa analysis for STRATFOR, a private security think tank based in Austin, Texas.

The attackers went cell by cell at the prison in Bauchi, breaking open locks and setting fire to part of the prison before escaping during the confusion with more than 750 inmates, said Bauchi state police commissioner Danlami Yar'Adua.

Five people a soldier, a police officer, two prison guards and a civilian died in the attack and six others remain in critical condition.

Members of Boko Haram rioted and attacked police stations and private homes in July 2009, triggering a violent police and military crackdown during which more than 700 people died. More than 120 followers arrested in the wake of the attacks last year were being held at the Bauchi prison pending trial.

Police believe the followers freed by the attack are now hiding in the mountains surrounding the pasturelands of the rural region.

"We have provided watertight security to hunt members of this group that we believe have not gone far," said Mohammed Barau, an assistant superintendent of police.

Bauchi remained calm Wednesday, as paramilitary police officers guarded the front of the damaged prison. They refused to allow an Associated Press reporter access the prison grounds. Footage later aired on the state-run Nigerian Television Authority showed piles of broken locks, burned-out rooms and a destroyed truck at the prison.

An unidentified official displays burnt equipment inside the Bauchi prison, September 9, 2010. (AP Photo/Sunday Alamba)

Police and military units added checkpoints along roads heading out of the city in hopes of catching escapees. Yar'Adua said his agency had arrested more than 20 suspected followers following the attack. Yar'Adua said 36 prisoners had returned to the prison on their own by Wednesday morning, hoping to serve out the remainder of their short sentences.

Boko Haram has campaigned for the implementation of strict Shariah law. Nigeria, a nation of 150 million people, is divided between the Christian-dominated south and the Muslim-held north. A dozen states across Nigeria's north already have Shariah law in place, though the area remains under the control of secular state governments.

In recent months, rumors about Boko Haram rearming have spread throughout northern Nigeria. A video recording released in late June showed a Boko Haram leader calling for new violence as the one-year anniversary of their attack neared. Meanwhile, police believe motorcycle-riding members of the sect are killing policemen in the region.

Cassette tapes of preaching by the sect once could be found across the north, said Mustapha Ismail, a Kano-based Islamic scholar writing a book about Boko Haram. Now, Nigeria's secret police arrest people for merely attempting to download sermons, forcing the group underground.

"With their members in so many jails and prisons, they are just trying to free them, at least for now," Ismail said.

The violence also comes as Nigeria's Jan. 22, 2011 presidential election nears. President Goodluck Jonathan, a Christian who took over after the death of elected Muslim leader Umaru Yar'Adua, has yet to say whether he'll run for office.

If Jonathan runs, it could anger the country's Muslim elite, who believe Yar'Adua would have won a second term under a power-sharing agreement in the nation's ruling party. Now Jonathan faces new pressure in trying to put down the sect without alienating Muslims or allowing security forces to conduct a violent reprisal like they did in 2009.

"He has to make a decision and his political enemies are going to use that against him either way," Schroeder said. "Either they'll say, 'OK, he's not being a strong commander in chief and he let violence get out of hand,' or he'll clamp down and that results in a large number of civilian casualties ... and they'll say, 'Jonathan is just another butcher and he's a butcher of northerners.'"

New Threats Invoke Al-Qaida
October 21, 2010
By Njadvara Musa

A Muslim sect suspected of a series of targeted killings and a massive prison break has issued new threats in northern Nigeria, this time invoking al-Qaida's North Africa branch.

Posters by the Boko Haram sect appeared at key intersections in the city of Maiduguri this week, bearing the name of Imam Abubakar Shekau, the group's de facto leader. The two top corners of the posters bore a symbol of an opened Quran, flanked on each side by Kalashnikov assault rifles and a flag in the middle mirroring the logo of al-Qaida in the Islamic Maghreb.

The message warned the public against assisting the police or going near soldiers guarding the town at night. The message also acknowledged a recent reward offered for information leading to the arrest of suspected sect members.

A Nigerian soldier, left, gestures as he and others show journalist arms, in Lagos, Nigeria, October 27, 2010. (AP Photo/Sunday Alamba, File)

"Any Muslim that goes against the establishment of Sharia (law) will be attacked and killed," the message read.

Boko Haram has campaigned for the implementation of strict Shariah law. Nigeria, a nation of 150 million people, is divided between the Christian-dominated south and the Muslim north. A dozen states across Nigeria's north already have Shariah law in place, though the area remains under the control of secular state governments.

The poster said it was from Shekau on behalf of "The Group of the People of Sunnah, Call and Jihad."

Police officers began removing the signs late Wednesday.

"These publications and messages on Boko Haram activities are seditious and could jeopardize our investigations into the four-month serial attacks and killings in the state," Borno state police commissioner Mohammed Abubakar said Thursday.

Authorities did not immediately comment on the use of the logos on the posters. Though the al-Qaida branch has distributed messages by Boko Haram before, it is unclear whether the two groups have any operational links. The two groups also come from two different ethnic groups in northern Nigeria.

Boko Haram sect members rioted and attacked police stations and private homes in July 2009, sparking a violent police and military crackdown. In total, 700 people died.

The sect largely went underground after the attack, though rumors began to spread this summer that the group was rearming. In September, authorities say Boko Haram members engineered an attack on a federal prison in Bauchi that freed about 750 inmates including imprisoned sect followers.

Meanwhile, suspected sect members on motorcycle taxis have killed politicians, religious leaders and police officers in recent weeks in Maiduguri and nearby cities. The killings have continued, despite the federal government sending soldiers to secure checkpoints throughout the region at night.

Concern of the killings, as well as recent car bombings in Nigeria's capital that killed at least 12, let the U.S. State Department to issue a new travel warning. The warning issued Tuesday urged U.S. citizens to avoid "all but essential travel" to Nigeria's oil-rich southern delta and regions inflamed by religious violence in central and northern Nigeria.

"Travelers throughout the country should be aware that, in areas where such circumstances prevail, there is the potential for ethnic or religious-based disturbances," the statement said.

Nigerians look at the burnt shells of cars after a car bomb exploded in Abuja as Nigeria celebrated its 50th independence anniversary, killing at least eight people in an unprecedented attack on the nation's capital, October 1, 2010. (AP Photo)

Boko Haram Stalks Northern Nigeria
December 18, 2010
By Jon Gambrell

In the dusty streets of northeastern Nigeria, far from the battlegrounds of Afghanistan, a group known as the Nigerian Taliban is waging war against a government it refuses to recognize.

The radical Muslim sect called Boko Haram was thought to be vanquished in 2009, when Nigeria's military crushed its mosque into concrete shards, and its leader was arrested and died in police custody. But now, a year later, Maiduguri and surrounding villages again live in fear of the group, whose members have assassinated police and local leaders and engineered a massive prison break, officials say.

Western diplomats are concerned that the sect is catching the attention of al-Qaida's North Africa branch. They also worry that Boko Haram represents chaos and disintegration in Nigeria, Africa's most populous nation and one of the top suppliers of crude oil to the United States.

"It is possible that Nigeria could be a future Pakistan," a leaked cable released by the WikiLeaks website quotes U.S. Assistant Secretary of African Affairs Johnnie Carson as saying earlier this year. "In 25 years, there could be impoverished masses, a wealthy elite and radicalism in the north. The question is whether the oil wells will be dry as well."

An unidentified man stands on the remains of the destroyed Boko Haram mosque in Maiduguri, Nigeria, November 12, 2010. (AP Photo/Sunday Alamba)

The cable later adds: "Nigeria is at a critical financial and political threshold and the entire nation could possibly tip backwards permanently."

Maiduguri sits in the upper northeast reaches of Nigeria, about 1,040 miles (1,675 kilometers) away from the country's commercial capital and seaport of Lagos. The sun rises as early as 6 a.m., quickly scorching the dusty streets and lands slowly being taken over by the growing Sahara Desert.

It was here a decade ago where Mohammed Yusuf, a one-time moderate imam, began preaching against the practices of Western education in life across Nigeria's Muslim north. Boko Haram was a constant refrain in the Hausa-language sermons, meaning "Western education is sacrilege."

Yusuf's words came at a time when about a dozen northern states adopted Islamic Shariah law, in the wake of the country becoming a democracy after decades of military dictatorships. Many believed the law, a code of conduct based on the teachings of the Quran, would end the corruption that gripped the country's government.

However, the Shariah courts remained under the control of secular state governments, which pushed them into roles of directing traffic and stopping beer trucks. Government continued as always, with politicians driving black luxury Land Rovers, and one trader boasted a mansion built for about $100 million, complete with a room plated in gold. In the meantime, more than 80 percent of the country's 150 million people lived on less than $2 a day.

Doyin Ajala plays inside an oil drum at the waterfront in Lagos, Nigeria, October 17, 2008. (AP Photo/Sunday Alamba)

"People are living in absolute poverty," said Ibrahim Ahmed Abdullahi, an imam in Maiduguri. "Whenever people are living in this type of poverty, if you start saying to them, 'Look, come let us bring about change,' ... people must listen to you."

University graduates who joined Boko Haram tore up their diplomas. Others joined riots in 2007 attacking police stations. Yusuf's preaching became even more incendiary.

In July 2009, sect members attacked local police stations and government buildings throughout northeast Nigeria. The riots brought a crackdown by Nigeria's military and left more than 700 dead. Yusuf himself died after he was captured by the military and turned over to police in a country where so-called "extrajudicial killings" by authorities remain the norm.

An overrun, grassy field is all that remains of Boko Haram's former headquarters, surrounded by the hulked, rusted remains of motorcycles and cars set ablaze during the group's last stand. The loudspeaker that once called members to prayers lies on the ground, silent, as paramilitary police pat down passers-by on motorcycle taxis and take palmed bribes from drivers.

But rumors began this year about the group rearming. A short time later, two-man teams on the back of the motorcycle taxis that fill Nigeria's streets began attacking police officers, religious leaders and local officials who had testified against the group in open court.

Women who fled following a deadly army attack on Ayakoromor village take refuge with other members of the community at a microcredit organization in the nearby town of Warri, Nigeria. The military launched a massive attack including aerial bombings that was aimed at finding a wanted militant. Civilians caught in the middle tried to escape with their lives, human rights activists say. The violence represents yet another example of how those toiling in poverty in a region that makes billions for Nigeria find themselves caught between a military seeking revenge and power-hungry militants, December 4, 2010. (AP Photo/Sunday Alamba)

In September, authorities say, Boko Haram members attacked a federal prison in Bauchi, freeing about 750 inmates with more than 100 belonging to the sect. It remains unclear how many members the group has in total.

Boko Haram members have amassed around Maiduguri, as well as across Nigeria's border with nearby Cameroon, Chad and Niger, said Borno state police spokesman Lawal Abdullahi. The group's swelling arms supply comes across Lake Chad and the expansive, poorly-patrolled bush that surrounds the city, Abdullahi said. The ancient trading routes that tied the region to Islam centuries ago now funnel weapons and foreign fighters to Boko Haram. The rise of Boko Haram stirred up fears not only in Maiduguri, but also in foreign embassies.

A secret diplomatic cable rounding up potential global threats was sent in June 2009 on behalf of U.S. Secretary of State Hillary Rodham Clinton, according to a copy recently released by WikiLeaks. The cable named Yusuf and identified his group as the "Nigerian Taliban." It warned that the group planned to launch a "massive surprise attack ... aimed at sparking sectarian clashes across Nigeria." The warning came a month before Boko Haram began its riot.

Diplomats also fear that Boko Haram may link with other foreign terror groups. After the 2009 violence, an arrested Boko Haram suspect told journalists he had been sent to Afghanistan to study bomb-making. His claim could not be independently verified.

In October, al-Qaida in the Islamic Maghreb, the North Africa branch of the terror group, apparently transmitted a Boko Haram message through an Internet forum on behalf of a Yusuf deputy now believed to be running the sect. In the June 2009 cable, the State Department also said a "well-trained veteran Chadian extremist" with "limited ties to al Qaida" had recently traveled to Nigeria. The cable said the man possibly came to raise money for a terror attack, but had no other information.

It remains unclear what, if any, formal links al-Qaida in the Islamic Maghreb has made with Boko Haram. The two groups belong to different ethnic groups with different customs. However, the al-Qaida group has paid local tribes in the past to take control of foreign hostages, and fighters linked to it have executed foreigners before.

History shows Maiduguri sits apart from the rest of the country. Though now a bookend of Nigeria's Muslim north, the region belonged to an ancient empire that stretched east rather than into the western Hausa lands. It remains insular even today.

Boko Haram took advantage of that, as well as the region's endemic poverty. The group's members likely come from the teeming poor in Nigeria and surrounding countries, said Murray Last, a professor emeritus of anthropology at the University College of London who studies Nigeria's north.

"What else would you actually do if you haven't got an education, if you haven't got a job, if you haven't got any future of a wife or a family?" Last asked. "Wouldn't it be better to join a religious community that might ensure you of a wife and children and sort of an education? ... A lot of young men have got no real option at all."

Many such young men flooded into northern Nigerian cities during the country's oil boom in the 1970s, hoping for jobs. Those coming from villages instead found hardship and alienation that made them receptive to any promise to change their lives, Last said.

That brought the north's first modern brush with Islamic extremism. Nigeria's north is dominated by Muslims, while its south is dominated by Christians.

Abdullahi Sule lifts homemade barbell weights, on a street in Maiduguri, Nigeria, November 12, 2010. (AP Photo/Sunday Alamba)

In 1980, the radical Maitatsine movement took hold in the ancient northern city of Kano. Led by a Cameroonian immigrant who inserted his own name into the Quran in place of the prophet Mohammed, the sect decried a corrupt federal government made up of "infidels." Riots left 4,000 people dead.

The military finally put down the sect after years of violence, but many still identified with the group.

"An awful lot of men and women sympathize with them," Last said. "One is dealing with an unspoken sense of: 'These people are thinking and doing things which may be wrong, but they aren't that far wrong.'"

Much remains murky about Boko Haram's intentions, and whether all the killings in Maiduguri are due to the group's reemergence. Local officials killed recently often had no previous ties with the group.

"They all can't be insurgent activity," said Abdullahi, the police spokesman.

Kaka Abubakar, a local government official, said he fought off gunmen barehanded whom authorities identified as Boko Haram members. However, when interviewed in front of his home guarded by three soldiers, he said he had no idea who his assailants were or what they wanted.

He walked quickly away down a quiet alley near his home, all of his neighbors watching. As an Associated Press reporter pulled out a notebook, a lance corporal guarding Abubakar's house shouted at him not to take notes.

"Please do not write anything down. Please do not ask questions," the soldier said. "These are innocent people."

Christmas Atrocities
December 27, 2010
By Njadvara Musa

Dozens of armed men attacked the church, dragging the pastor out of his home and shooting him to death. Two young men from the choir rehearsing for a late-night carol service also were slain.

The group of about 30 attackers armed with guns and knives even killed two people passing by Victory Baptist Church. The assailants only left after setting the church and pastor's house ablaze.

Danjuma Akawu, the church's secretary, managed to escape after he and others climbed over the church's fence.

"I cannot understand these attacks," Akawu said. "Why Christians? Why Christians? The police have failed to protect us."

At the opposite end of the city, Rev. Haskanda Jessu said that three men attacked the Church of Christ in Nigeria an hour later, killing a 60-year-old security guard.

At least 38 people died in Christmas Eve attacks across Nigeria, including the six killed at churches in the country's north by suspected members of a radical Muslim sect. In central Nigeria, 32 died in a series of bomb blasts in the worst violence to hit the region in months.

Authorities have not identified suspects following the Christmas Eve explosions in Jos and it was not immediately clear if those attacks had a religious motive. Two of the bombs went off near a large market where people were doing last-minute Christmas shopping. A third hit a mainly Christian area of Jos, while the fourth was near a road that leads to the city's main mosque.

Bystanders gather around a burned car outside the Victory Baptist Church in Maiduguri. Authorities say dozens of assailants attacked the church on Christmas Eve, killing the pastor, two members of the choir and two people passing by the church. Police are blaming members of Boko Haram, December 25, 2010. (AP Photo - Njadvara Musa)

On Sunday, there were reports of renewed violence in the area, though no official figures were released on the number of people who may have been wounded or killed.

Police have not said whether they believe the bombings were related to the church attacks. The two areas are about 320 miles (520 kilometers) apart.

The group blamed for the church attacks the radical Muslim sect known as Boko Haram used to be based in Bauchi, about 75 miles (120 kilometers) from the area where the bombs went off. The group is now headquartered in Maiduguri, where the church attacks took place.

The African Union Commission's Chairman, Jean Ping, expressed shock and sadness at the explosions in Jos and church attacks in Maiduguri.

"He condemns in the strongest terms these cowardly terrorist attacks, which cannot be justified under any circumstances," said a statement released by his office Sunday.

Nigerian President Goodluck Jonathan has expressed his sympathy to the victims' families and said the government will bring the perpetrators to justice.

"I assure Nigerians that government will go to the root of this," he said of the explosions. "We must unearth what caused it and those behind it must be brought to book."

The United Nations spokesman's office said Secretary-General Ban Ki-Moon condemned the violence in Nigeria "especially at a time when millions of Nigerians are celebrating religious holidays."

Ban "supports efforts by the Nigerian authorities to bring those responsible to justice," the spokesman's office said, and "conveys his sincere condolences to the families of the victims and to the Government and people of the Federal Republic of Nigeria."

Religious violence already has left more than 500 people dead this year in Jos and neighboring towns and villages, but the situation was believed to have calmed down before the weekend bombings. The explosions Friday were the first major attack in Jos since the state government lifted a curfew in May.

The curfew had first been imposed in November 2008 during postelection violence but it was extended in January following clashes between Christian and Muslim groups. More than 300 people mostly Muslims were killed in the January violence in Jos and surrounding villages.

Nigeria, a country of 150 million people, is almost evenly split between Muslims in the north and the predominantly Christian south. The blasts happened in central Nigeria, in the nation's "middle belt," where dozens of ethnic groups vie for control of fertile lands.

The violence, though fractured across religious lines, often has more to do with local politics, economics and rights to grazing lands. The government of Plateau state, where Jos is the capital, is controlled by Christian politicians who have blocked Muslims from being legally recognized as citizens. That has locked many out of prized government jobs in a region where the tourism industry and tin mining have collapsed in the last decades.

Police and the army have declined to identify suspects in the Jos bombings, and state governor David Jang would only say "we believe some highly placed people masterminded the attack." Authorities, though, already have blamed the radical Muslim sect Boko Haram for the Christmas Eve church attacks.

The radical Muslim sect was thought to be vanquished in 2009. Nigeria's military crushed its mosque into concrete shards, and its leader was arrested and died in police custody.

In this image made from video provided NTA via APTN, a burned out van is seen on a road following violence in Jos, Nigeria. Dozens of people were killed over the holiday weekend in attacks across Nigeria, including 32 who died in central Nigeria in a series of bomb blasts in the worst violence to hit the region in months, December 25, 2010. (AP Photo/NTA via APTN)

But now, a year later, Maiduguri and surrounding villages again live in fear of the group, whose members have assassinated police and local leaders and engineered a massive prison break, officials say. Western diplomats worry that the sect is catching the attention of al-Qaida's North Africa branch. It remains unclear what, if any, formal links al-Qaida in the Islamic Maghreb has made with Boko Haram.

The holiday violence in Nigeria comes as the president, a Christian from the south of Nigeria, is trying to unify the country to support him ahead of next year's election. Jonathan became president earlier this year following the death of Nigeria's elected Muslim leader, and some within his party feel the next leader should also be Muslim.

Party leaders had anticipated that Jonathan's predecessor would hold office for two, four-year terms like the Christian president before him. An unwritten agreement in the ruling People's Democratic Party calls for its presidential candidates to alternate between the Christian south and the Muslim north.

New Year's Eve Bombing
December 31, 2010
By Bashir Adigun and Jon Gambrell

A bomb blast tore through a beer garden at a Nigerian army barracks where revelers had gathered to celebrate New Year's Eve, witnesses said, and state-run television reported Friday (December 31) that 30 people died, though police immediately disputed that.

A local police spokesman said the blast occurred at about 7:30 p.m. Friday in Abuja, the capital of Africa's most populous nation.

No one immediately claimed responsibility for the explosion in this oil-rich nation where citizens remain uneasy after bombings at other locations had killed dozens of people several days earlier.

"It's unfortunate that some people planted (a) bomb where people are relaxing because of the new year," Air Marshal Oluseyi Petirin told journalists. "Nobody has been able to give accurate figures (of casualties), but we have rescued some people."

An anchor on the state-run Nigerian Television Authority gave a death toll of 30 to viewers Friday night. The channel did not give an estimate on the number of injured.

Local police spokesman Jimoh Moshood immediately disputed the figure, saying only four people had died and 13 were wounded. Death tolls remain contentious in Nigeria, as politicians often inflate or shrink tolls to suit their aspirations.

Witnesses said the market appeared full at the time of the blast. A local journalist at the scene told The Associated Press that soldiers carried injured people away, with one officer saying he feared there were fatalities.

In the minutes after the explosion, police and soldiers swarmed the area, blocking onlookers from entering the area. Later, an AP journalist saw police carrying out covered bodies and putting them in the back of police vehicles. Officers shouted at each other to keep the bodies covered and hidden from onlookers.

The base, called the Mogadishu Cantonment, includes an area of market stalls and beer parlors referred to locally as a "mammy market." There, civilians and soldiers regularly gather for drinks and its famous barbecued fish.

The blasts come days after a similar attack struck a nation that remains uneasily divided between Christians and Muslims. On Christmas Eve, three bombs exploded in the central Nigerian city of Jos, killing dozens of people. That area has seen more than 500 die in religious and ethnic violence this year alone.

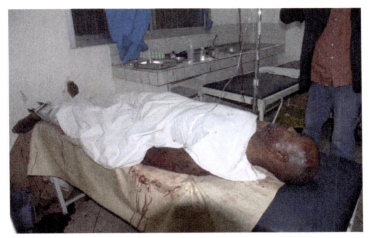

A victim of a bomb explosion lying on a bed in the Asokoro General Hospital, Abuja, Nigeria. A bomb blast tore through a beer garden at a Nigerian army barracks where revelers had gathered to celebrate New Year's Eve, witnesses said, and state-run television reported that 30 people died, December 31, 2010. (AP Photo/Felix Onigbinde)

Members of a radical Muslim sect attacked two churches in the northern city of Maiduguri the same night, killing at least six people.

The sect, known locally as Boko Haram, later claimed responsibility for both attacks in an Internet message. Police say they are still investigating those attacks.

Boko Haram's members re-emerged recently after starting a July 2009 riot that led to a security crackdown that left 700 people dead.

The Christmas Eve killings in Jos and Maiduguri add to the tally of thousands who already have died in Nigeria in the last decade over religious and political tension. The bombings also come as the nation prepares for what could be a tumultuous presidential election in April.

This isn't the first time Nigeria's typically quiet capital has seen violence this year. A dual car bombing killed at least 12 people and wounded dozens more during an Oct. 1 independence celebration in the capital. The main militant group in Nigeria's oil-rich southern delta, the Movement for the Emancipation of the Niger Delta, claimed responsibility for the attack.

In a statement, a spokesman for President Goodluck Jonathan said whoever planted the bomb wanted "to turn the joys of fellow Nigerians to ashes."

"This is extreme evil. It is wicked. It defies all that we believe in and stand for as a nation," the statement from Ima Niboro read.

It added: "They must be made to pay. No one, and we repeat, no one, can make this nation ungovernable."

Nigeria, an OPEC-member nation, remains a vital supplier of easily refined crude oil to the U.S. Unrest in the West African nation has affected oil prices in the past. Beyond that, Western diplomats worry ethnic, religious and political violence could hobble the nation of 150 million people forever just as it adjusts to democracy after years of military dictatorships and coups.

3

Goodluck Jonathan

Nigerian President Goodluck Jonathan, center, inspects a guard of honor during his inauguration ceremony at the main parade ground in Nigeria's capital of Abuja, Sunday. Jonathan was sworn in for a full four-year term as president of Nigeria and is now faced with the challenge of uniting a country that saw deadly postelection violence despite what observers called the fairest vote in over a decade, May 29, 2011. (AP Photo/Sunday Alamba)

Goodluck Jonathan Win Brings Riots
April 18, 2011
By Jon Gambrell

Nigerian President Goodluck Jonathan won the oil-rich country's election Monday as riots swept across the Muslim north and left buildings ablaze and people hiding in their homes, highlighting the religious and ethnic tensions still dividing Africa's most populous nation.

The violence cut across 13 states, hundreds wounded. Heavy gunfire echoed through cities, as shouting crowds burned tires and threw stones at security forces. Many were feared dead, though federal officials declined to offer any figures for fear of further stoking tensions.

In a televised address to the nation late Monday (April 18), Jonathan called on Nigerians to "quickly move away from partisan battlegrounds and find a national common ground."

"Nobody's political ambition is worth the blood of any Nigerian," he said, hours after police said an angry mob in Katsina state engineered a prison break.

While Christians and Muslims have shared the same soil in the nation for centuries, the election result showing the Christian president's more than 10 million vote lead over Muslim candidate Muhammadu Buhari spread accusations of rigging in a nation long accustomed to ballot box stuffing.

Gen. Muhammadu Buhari, presidential candidate of the Congress for Progressive Change, attends a campaign rally in Lagos, Nigeria. Buhari, a former military ruler of Nigeria, has gained support in his third bid to become president of the oil-rich nation. Buhari ruled Nigeria from 1983 to 1985 after a military coup deposed the elected president, April 6, 2011. (AP Photo/Sunday Alamba)

Jonathan took office last year only after the country's elected Muslim president died from a lengthy illness before his term ended, and many in the north still believe the ruling party should have put up a Muslim candidate instead in this year's election.

"The damage is immense. A lot of buildings have been torched: houses, businesses and religious centers," said Umar Mairiga of the Nigerian Red Cross.

More than 270 people had been wounded and some 15,000 had been displaced by the violence, he said.

Nigeria has a long history of violent and rigged polls since it abandoned a revolving door of military rulers and embraced democracy 12 years ago. Legislative elections earlier this month left a hotel ablaze, a politician dead and a polling station and a vote-counting center bombed in the nation's northeast. However, observers largely said Saturday's presidential election appeared to be fair, with fewer cases of ballot box thefts than previous polls.

Election chairman Attahiru Jega announced results Monday night that showed Jonathan won 22.4 million votes, compared to the 12.2 million votes of his nearest rival, the former military ruler Buhari. Jonathan also received enough votes across Nigeria's 36 states and capital to avoid triggering a runoff. The West African nation of 150 million people is divided between a Christian-dominated south and the Muslim north.

A dozen states across Nigeria's north have Islamic Shariah law in place, though they remain under the control of secular state governments. Thousands have been killed in religious violence in the past decade, but the roots of the sectarian conflict are often embedded in struggles for political and economic dominance.

People wait to cast their vote by a house destroyed house in post election violence, during gubernatorial elections, in Kaduna, Nigeria. Small crowds of voters nervously cast ballots in two states in oil-rich Nigeria hit hard by religious rioting that killed at least 500 people following the nation's presidential election, April 28, 2011. (AP Photo/Sunday Alamba)

Buhari carried northern states where poverty remains endemic and opportunities few. Many there supported Buhari, a disciplinarian who took power after a 1983 New Year's Eve coup, as his campaign promised change in a nation ruled by the same ruling political party since it became a democracy.

Buhari's party brought a formal complaint against the nation's electoral commission even before the vote count ended, alleging massive rigging in Jonathan's homeland of the Niger Delta. The letter also alleged that the computer software used to tally results had been tampered with in northern states to favor the ruling People's Democratic Party.

"What is being exhibited to the world is not collated from polling units but ... a lot of manipulations," the letter read.

Both Buhari's party and the opposition party Action Congress of Nigeria refused to sign off on the results.

Violence began Sunday in the north, but took full hold Monday morning. Witnesses said youths in the northern city of Kano set fires to homes that bore Jonathan party banners. Heavy gunfire also could be heard. An Associated Press reporter there saw hundreds of youths carrying wooden planks in the street, shouting "Only Buhari" in the local Hausa language.

"What I am looking for now is rescue, the mob is still outside. I need rescue," said Mark Asu-Obi, who was trapped inside his Kano home with his wife and three children. "There are hoodlums all over the place. It's not just my place that they are attacking. I am not a politician. I am an independent observer."

In Kaduna, home to the oil-rich nation's vice president, angry young men burned tires in the streets and threw stones at police and soldiers trying to restore order, witnesses said. Youths targeted ruling party officials in Bauchi state as well.

"All of you came out in the sun and elected the person after your heart, I thank you for doing that but let us remain peaceful in all our conducts so that we will not be plunged into a crisis situation in the state," Bauchi state Gov. Isa Yuguda said in a statewide radio and television broadcast.

The violence did not affect Nigeria's oil-rich southern delta, where foreign companies pump more than 2 million barrels of crude a day out of a country crucial to U.S. gasoline supplies. A statement attributed to former militant leaders there warned they would defend Jonathan's mandate "with the last drop of our blood." The statement said leaders also ordered fighters to return to the delta's winding muddy creeks to await instructions.

A Soldier stands guard as voters cast their ballots during the gubernatorial election in Kaduna. Two states in Nigeria's Muslim north voted for state gubernatorial candidates after their polls were delayed by violence that killed at least 500 last week after the oil-rich nation's presidential election, April 28, 2011. (AP Photo/Sunday Alamba)

Jonathan came to power after the May 2010 death of Nigeria's long-ill elected leader, President Umaru Yar'Adua. Still, many in Nigeria's Muslim north remain uneasy about Jonathan, a Christian from the country's south. The north's elite political class wanted the ruling party to honor an unwritten power-sharing agreement that would have placed another northern candidate into the presidency. However, Jonathan ultimately prevailed in a ruling party primary.

Violence Follows Inauguration
May 30, 2011
By Shehu Saulawa

Multiple blasts rocked Nigeria's restive Muslim north and a city near the capital following the inauguration of the country's southern Christian president, officials said Monday (May 30).

The most powerful of the blasts tore through a bar in a military barracks in the northern city of Bauchi on Sunday, killing 15 people just hours after the swearing-in ceremony, said an official who participated in the rescue efforts.

Bauchi state police chief Mohammed Indabawa said Sunday's blast in the city of Bauchi hit an outdoor bar at about 8 p.m., just hours after the inauguration of President Goodluck Jonathan in Nigeria's capital of Abuja.

Indabawa said 10 people were killed, but the official who helped emergency workers take victims to the hospital and to the mortuary said 15 people were killed and 35 injured. He said he didn't want his name used because the military has said that this is a military affair.

An Associated Press writer who was about 1,300 feet (400 meters) from the Shadawanka Barracks when the blasts went off said he heard three consecutive loud noises at two- to five-minute intervals.

The multiple blasts illustrate the challenges facing Jonathan. The southerner was sworn in Sunday for a full four-year term and is now faced with the task of uniting a country that saw deadly postelection violence despite what observers called the fairest vote in more than a decade.

A spokesman for the National Emergency Management Agency, Yushau Shuaib, said stringent security measures had been taken to prevent such attacks on inauguration day.

"Telecommunications operators blocked service in Abuja yesterday and government took so many other measures to prevent this, but it is unfortunate that this still happened," he said. "The Agency moved in quickly, otherwise this would have been even worse."

One bomb went off Sunday at a beer garden in Zuba, near Nigeria's capital, killing two people and wounding at least 11, Shuaib said.

Another explosion in the northern city of Zaria on Sunday also targeted a bar hours after the inauguration, police spokesman Aminu Lawal said. He said police were still looking into how many may have been wounded in that blast.

And on Monday, two teenagers were injured after stepping on explosives in Zaria, Lawal said.

In the northeast city of Maiduguri, a bomb targeted on Monday an army patrol vehicle, Lt. Abubakar Abdullahi said, adding that there were no casualties and five arrests were made after the incident.

No one has claimed responsibility for any of the blasts.

"For now we are trying to gather intelligence on the perpetrators, make sure the victims are attended to, and investigate the matter," national police spokesman Olusola Amore said of the blasts around the country.

The nation of 150 million people with more than 150 ethnic groups is broadly divided between the Christian-dominated south and the Muslim north. Postelection violence spread quickly across northern states after early results showed that Jonathan, a Christian from the south, was winning.

Local Chiefs from the Niger Delta, attend the inauguration ceremony of Nigerian President Goodluck Jonathan at the main parade ground in Nigeria's capital of Abuja. Goodluck Jonathan was sworn in for a full four-year term as president of Nigeria and is now faced with the challenge of uniting a country that saw deadly postelection violence, May 29, 2011. (AP Photo/Sunday Alamba)

Many northerners believed someone from their region should be the next leader after the Muslim president died in office. Late President Yar'Adua had been expected to rule for another term, but his death left the presidency in the hands of a southerner. An unwritten agreement in the ruling party calls for its presidential candidates to rotate between the country's Christian south and Muslim north.

Bauchi city has a history of sectarian violence and was a scene of rioting and destruction after the April elections.

Bauchi is also a stronghold of a radical Muslim sect locally known as Boko Haram. Its members are accused of a rash of killings in the area in recent months which have targeted police officers, soldiers and political and spiritual leaders.

Boko Haram, which means "Western education is sacrilege" in the Hausa language, has asked pushed for the implementation of Sharia law in northern states.

Authorities blame the group for an explosion at a hotel in April that killed three people and wounded 14 others in Maiduguri, a city close to Bauchi, only days before the state's gubernatorial election.

Tensions in Nigeria are fueled by poverty and unemployment in a country where an unreliable power supply has led to the closure of factories and the loss of tens of thousands of jobs in the textile industry alone over the last few years, especially in the Muslim north.

Boko Haram Begins Suicide Bombings
June 18, 2011
By Yinka Ibukun

The radical Muslim sect has shot police officials and clerics from atop motorcycles, torched churches and even freed hundreds in a brazen prison escape in Nigeria's restive north. But this week, Boko Haram expanded its reach and claimed its first suicide bombing in the capital of Africa's most populous nation.

Fire fighters, put out a fire following an explosion, at the police headquarters, in Abuja. A suicide bombing in the parking lot of police headquarters killed two people, police said. Olusola Amore, national police spokesman, told journalists that two people were confirmed dead after a car blew up in the parking lot outside the building of the police headquarters, June 16, 2011. (AP Photo/Felix Onigbinde)

Thursday's (June 16) attack killed at least two people and sent a thick cloud of smoke into the sky that could be seen from across the capital. By striking at the national police headquarters in Abuja, analysts say the group is showing it is willing to spread its fight beyond Nigeria's Muslim-dominated north.

"This was a bold and deliberate statement on their part to announce that they have come to stay," said criminologist and security consultant Innocent Chukwuma.

Boko Haram, whose name in the local Hausa language means "Western education is sacrilege," has long campaigned for the implementation of strict Shariah law across Nigeria's northern states. The country's south is predominantly Christian.

The group is responsible for a rash of killings which have targeted security officers, politicians and clerics in Nigeria's northeast over the last year. But until recently, most attacks have been near the sect's stronghold of Maiduguri, about 540 miles (some 880 kilometers) from Abuja.

Author Shehu Sani, who wrote "The Killing Fields," an account of religious violence in Nigeria, says the government has long denied the severity of the situation.

"The truth is that Nigeria is engaged in a deadly Islamic insurgency which the authorities are continuously denying and downplaying," he said.

Western governments have previously expressed concern over Boko Haram, with the U.S. calling the group the "Nigerian Taliban" in a 2009 cable released last year by the WikiLeaks website.

The documents also expressed fear that Boko Haram was catching the attention of al-Qaida's North African branch.

In a leaflet attributed to the group and delivered to journalists Wednesday, Boko Haram claimed that some of its members had been trained in Somalia. The lack of an effective government there has allowed terror groups to operate freely.

"Very soon," the message said in Hausa, "we will wage Jihad on the enemies of God and His Prophet."

It became clear Boko Haram had broadened its reach in May, after a man who said he spoke for the group claimed responsibility for multiple blasts that hit beer gardens in two northern cities and a town near the capital, leaving 18 people dead.

The May 29 attacks came hours after Nigeria inaugurated President Goodluck Jonathan.

Burned out cars, at the parking lot of the police headquarters in Abuja, June 16, 2011. (AP Photo/Felix Onigbinde)

Jonathan then expressed his readiness to negotiate with Nigeria's new crop of militants. Militancy in the country's oil-rich delta had already been appeased with a 2009 amnesty program. The governor of the state most affected by Boko Haram attacks made a similar offer to the sect.

But the group seemed unwilling to cooperate. In leaflet distributed June 12 and signed by a man called Usman Al-Zawahiri, they imposed a laundry list of conditions that they said needed to be met before they would enter talks the government. That list included the implementation of Shariah law in the north, the resignation of the newly elected state government and the prosecution of top officials who the group holds responsible for the death of Boko Haram leader Mohammed Yusuf, who died in police custody in 2009.

Shortly after those demands were made, Inspector General of Police Hafiz Ringim visited the Boko Haram stronghold of Maiduguri. During Tuesday's visit, he said the group's days were "numbered."

Two days later, the suicide bomber attacked just outside Ringim's office. A traffic warden was the only confirmed death, aside from the alleged bomber.

Jonathan, in a bid to reassure Nigerians, said Friday that "security agencies are on top of it," as he stood amid the wreckage in the parking lot of what many Nigerians consider a bastion of security.

He asked people not to panic, adding that such attacks would soon be "a thing of the past."

But people say they are not reassured.

"This was not an ordinary police station," said Chukwuma Awaegbu, a 36 year-old fashion designer in the commercial capital of Lagos. "It was the police headquarters for the whole country ... Anything can happen, anything, anytime, anywhere."

Nigerian security forces lack the tools to prevent serious security threats, said Chukwuma, the security consultant.

"Their reform has emphasized more on hardware at the expense of investment in intelligence-led approaches," he said.

In Maiduguri, residents say the police's heavy-handed approach is not working.

"The police should stop killing sect members," said 52-year-old Umaru Giwi on Saturday. "They should prosecute the arrested ones in court instead of killing them on the battlefield."

As security agencies struggle to fight back, analysts say Boko Haram's tactics keep evolving.

"Suicide bombing is a culture," said Olusegun Sotola, a researcher at the Lagos-based Institute for Public Policy Analysis. "It has become entrenched in other parts of the world, and it can take root here too."

United Nations Bombed in Nigeria's Capital
August 27, 2011
By Jon Gambrell

Nigeria will bring terrorism "under control" and confront the radical Muslim sect that claimed responsibility for a car bombing at the country's United Nations headquarters, killing at least 19 people, its president vowed Saturday (August 27) amid the wreckage.

President Goodluck Jonathan stepped through shattered glass and past dried pools of blood at the damaged building as U.N. employees salvaged printers, computers and all they could carry to keep the mission running.

The U.N.'s top official in Nigeria promised humanitarian aid would continue to flow through the world body to Africa's most populous nation, even though the Boko Haram sect which claimed responsibility for the attack views it as a target.

Debris and security tape surround the Nigerian headquarters of the United Nations one day after a suicide bomber crashed through an exit gate and into the reception area detonating a car full of explosives and killing least 19 people, August 27, 2011. (AP Photo/Rebecca Blackwell)

"I think it gives us more strength to continue helping the population," said Agathe Lawson, the U.N.'s acting resident coordinator in Nigeria.

Meanwhile, a spokesman for the feared sect told journalists Saturday in its home of northeast Nigeria that it considers the U.S, the U.N. and the Nigerian government the "common enemies" in its fight, promising future attacks.

Jonathan walked by the battered exit gate the suicide bomber rammed through to reach the massive U.N. building's glass reception hall Friday morning.

There, the bomber detonated explosives powerful enough to bring down parts of the concrete structure and blow out glass windows from other buildings in the quiet neighborhood filled with diplomatic posts.

A bevy of bodyguards, police, soldiers and members of the country's secret police surrounded Jonathan on his tour. The soft-spoken president promised journalists gathered there that the nation would stand up to terrorism, though Boko Haram continues to carry out bombings and assassinations seemingly at will.

"Terrorist attacks on any individual or part of the world is a terrorist attack on the rest of the world," Jonathan said. "Terrorists don't care about who is anywhere."

Jonathan did not say who was responsible for the attack, only addressing Boko Haram in response to a reporter's question.

Nigeria President Goodluck Jonathan, center, speaks to journalists after visiting the explosion site at the United Nation's office after a car blew up in Abuja. Nigeria's president says his government will bring terrorism "under control," August 27, 2011. (AP Photo/Sunday Alamba)

"Boko Haram is a local group linked up with terrorist activities," the president said. "As a government, we are working on this and we will bring it under control."

The president did not elaborate on that comment, as his aides hustled him off into a convoy of armored Mercedes Benz sedans, police trucks and motorcycles.

The death toll for the attack rose to 19 on Saturday, said Yushau Shuaib, a spokesman for Nigeria's National Emergency Management Agency. At least

15 of the dead were U.N. personnel, U.N. deputy spokesman Farhan Haq said Friday night from New York.

However, a U.N. statement sent Saturday from the Nigeria office said nine U.N. staffers were confirmed dead and dozens were hospitalized.

The National Hospital in Abuja alone treated 75 injured people from the bomb blast Friday, said Obasi Ekumankama, the hospital's director of clinical services.

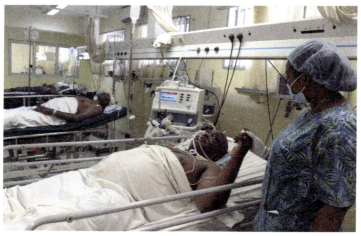

A World Health Organization employee, injured in the suicide attack on U.N. headquarters, is comforted by a hospital worker as he recovers alongside other blast victims in the intensive care unit of the national hospital in Abuja. The death toll from the car bombing has risen to 23, a U.N. spokesman said, making the attack one of the deadliest on the U.N. in a decade, August 28, 2011. (AP Photo/Rebecca Blackwell, Pool)

The U.N. had yet to complete a head count of its staff at the building, which houses about 400 workers, Lawson said.

A U.N. team that includes Deputy Secretary-General Asha-Rose Migiro and security chief Gregory Starr was expected to arrive in Abuja late Saturday night. But other help is already being given by the international community: A U.S. embassy car carrying what local authorities described as FBI agents arrived at the bomb site a short time after Jonathan left.

Deb MacLean, a spokeswoman for the U.S. embassy in Abuja, said FBI agents "were on the ground" to assist after the bombing. She declined to elaborate.

Security appeared tighter than normal in Abuja, about 550 miles (880 kilometers) northeast of the country's megacity of Lagos. Soldiers wearing flak jackets blocked the main highway heading into the city from Abuja's international airport Saturday morning, checking passing vehicles.

Friday's bombing represented the first suicide attack targeting foreigners by Boko Haram, whose name means "Western education is sacrilege" in the local Hausa language. The group, which has reported links to al-Qaida, wants to implement a strict version of Shariah law in the nation and is vehemently opposed to Western education and culture. It claimed responsibility for a similar car bombing at the country's federal police headquarters in Abuja in June that killed at least two people.

Earlier this month, the commander for U.S. military operations in Africa told The Associated Press that Boko Haram may be trying to coordinate attacks with two al-Qaida-linked groups, al-Qaida in the Islamic Maghreb, which operates in northwest Africa, and al-Shabab in Somalia.

A Nairobi-based diplomat told the AP on Saturday that at least 19 Nigerians had arrived late in 2010 and stayed with Somali Islamist militia al-Shabab in the house of a former Somali general in the rebel-held part of Mogadishu until April. Several of them were believed to be members of Boko Haram, the diplomat said.

An unidentified woman, who reportedly lost her husband in last month's suicide attack on United Nations headquarters, weeps during a memorial service for those killed, outside the damaged building. U.N. officials have joined diplomats and Nigeria's foreign minister in remembering the 23 people killed in the car bombing of the world body's office, September 15, 2011. (AP Photo/Felix Onigbinde)

The diplomat spoke on condition of anonymity because he was not authorized to speak to the press.

The sect itself spoke out to journalists gathered Saturday in the city of Maiduguri, its home before members started a 2009 riot that saw a security crackdown that left 700 people dead. A man who identified himself as Abu Kakah told journalists in a telephone interview that the sect continued to launch attacks because of the government's harassment of its members.

Unidentified members of Oodua People's Congress militia ride on buses carrying guns and machetes during a protest against Boko Haram in Lagos, Nigeria. The militia group from Nigeria's southwest walked through the streets of the commercial capital firing rifles as police and security forces fled. The group said they were protesting the rise of Boko Haram, December 8, 2011. (AP Photo/Sunday Alamba)

"We attacked and bombed the U.N. offices in Abuja because the United States and U.N. are both fully supporting the federal government of Nigeria in persecuting and attacking Muslims all over the country with no cause or justification," Kakah said in Hausa. He later promised future attacks in the north, saying the sect would release information soon about the suicide bomber who attacked the U.N. headquarters.

On Saturday, U.N. employees milled around the outside of the damaged headquarters, some wiping away tears. One woman spoke of a relative she believed was dead and buried amid the rubble.

Lawson, the U.N.'s acting resident coordinator, said workers already set up another office to continue their work, though much more space was needed to carry out the body's work. Nigeria, a country of 150 million people largely split between a Christian south and Muslim north, remains desperately poor after decades of oil wealth being squandered by its political elite.

The U.N. will continue to provide food and health care to the nation's teeming poor despite the bombing, Lawson said.

Now, however, the international body needs assistance as well.

"We prepared," Lawson said, facing the broken building's giant "U.N. Cares" banner. "Security was in place, but it is never enough."

Suspected members of Boko Haram enter the federal High court before their arraignment hearing in Abuja, where they are accused of plotting bombings that killed 25 people in Nigeria. The six appeared in court over the killings and they have pleaded not guilty to the charges, September 23, 2011. (AP Photo/Dele Jo)

More Christmas Bombings
December 26, 2011
By Lekan Oyekanmi and Jon Gambrell

Women returned to clean the blood from St. Theresa Catholic Church on Monday (December 26) and one man wept uncontrollably amid its debris as a Nigerian Christian association demanded protection for its churches.

At least 35 people died at St. Theresa and dozens more were wounded as radical Muslim militants launched coordinated attacks across Africa's most populous nation within hours of one another. Four more people were killed in other violence blamed on the group known as Boko Haram.

Crowds gathered among the burned-out cars in the church's dirt parking lot Monday, angry over the attack and fearful that the group will target more of their places of worship.

It was the second year in a row that the extremists seeking to install Islamic Shariah law across the country of 160 million staged such attacks. Last year, a series of bombings on Christmas Eve killed 32 people in Nigeria.

Rev. Father Christopher Jataudarde told The Associated Press that Sunday's blast happened as church officials gave parishioners white powder as part of a tradition celebrating the birth of Christ. Some already had left the church at the time of the bombing, causing the massive casualties.

Onlookers gather around a car destroyed in a blast next to St. Theresa Catholic Church in Madalla, Nigeria. An explosion ripped through the Catholic church during Christmas Mass killing scores of people, December 25, 2011. (AP Photo/Sunday Aghaeze)

In the ensuing chaos, a mortally wounded man had cradled his wounded stomach and begged a priest for religious atonement. "Father, pray for me. I will not survive," he said.

At least 52 people were wounded in the blast, said Slaku Luguard, a coordinator with Nigeria's National Emergency Management Agency. Victims filled the cement floors of a nearby government hospital, some crying in pools of their own blood.

Pope Benedict XVI denounced the bombing at his post-Christmas blessing Monday, urging people to pray for the victims and Nigeria's Christian community.

"In this moment, I want to repeat once again with force: Violence is a path that leads only to pain, destruction and death. Respect, reconciliation and love are the only path to peace," he said.

Blood stains of a victim of the bomb blast are seen at St. Theresa Catholic Church, December 25, 2011. (AP Photo/Sunday Agaeze)

The U.N. Security Council condemned the attacks "in the strongest terms" and called for the perpetrators, organizers, financiers and sponsors "of these reprehensible acts" to be brought to justice.

The African Union also condemned the attacks and pledged to support Nigeria in its fight against terrorism.

"Boko Haram's continued acts of terror and cruelty and absolute disregard for human life cannot be justified by any religion or faith," said a statement attributed to AU commission chairman Jean Ping.

On Sunday, a bomb also exploded amid gunfire in the central Nigeria city of Jos and a suicide car bomber attacked the military in the nation's northeast. Three people died in those assaults.
After the bombings, a Boko Haram spokesman using the nom de guerre Abul-Qaqa claimed responsibility for the attacks in an interview with The

Daily Trust, the newspaper of record across Nigeria's Muslim north. The sect has used the newspaper in the past to communicate with public.

"There will never be peace until our demands are met," the newspaper quoted the spokesman as saying. "We want all our brothers who have been incarcerated to be released; we want full implementation of the Sharia system and we want democracy and the constitution to be suspended."

Boko Haram has carried out increasingly sophisticated and bloody attacks in its campaign to implement strict Shariah law across Nigeria. The group is responsible for at least 504 killings this year alone, according to an Associated Press count.

Onlookers gather around a destroyed car at the site of the bomb blast at St. Theresa Catholic Church, December 25, 2011. (AP Photo/Sunday Aghaeze)

Last year, a series of Christmas Eve bombings in Jos claimed by the militants left at least 32 dead and 74 wounded. The group also claimed responsibility for the Aug. 26 bombing of the United Nations headquarters in Nigeria's capital Abuja that killed 24 people and wounded 116 others.

While initially targeting enemies via hit-and-run assassinations from the back of motorbikes after the 2009 riot, violence by Boko Haram now has a new sophistication and apparent planning that includes high-profile attacks with greater casualties.

That has fueled speculation about the group's ties as it has splintered into at least three different factions, diplomats and security sources say. They say the more extreme wing of the sect maintains contact with terror groups in North Africa and Somalia.

Mourners and priests gather in the back lot of a Catholic church turned into a mass grave for the dead killed in a Christmas Day bombing in Madalla, February 1, 2012. (AP Photo/Sunday Aghaeze, File)

Targeting Boko Haram has remained difficult, as sect members are scattered throughout northern Nigeria and the nearby countries of Cameroon, Chad and Niger. Analysts say political considerations also likely play a part in the country's thus-far muted response: President Goodluck Jonathan, a Christian from the south, may be hesitant to use force in the nation's predominantly Muslim north. Speaking late Sunday at a prayer service, Jonathan described the bombing as an "ugly incident." "There is no reason for these kind of dastardly acts," the president said in a ceremony aired by the state-run Nigerian Television Authority. "It's one of the burdens as a nation we have to carry. We believe it will not last forever."

However, others don't remain as sure as the president. The northern state section of the powerful Christian Association of Nigeria issued a statement late Monday night demanding government protection for its churches, warning that "the situation may degenerate to a religious war."

"We shall henceforth in the midst of these provocations and wanton destruction of innocent lives and property be compelled to make our own efforts and arrangements to protect the lives of innocent Christians and peace loving citizens of this country," the statement read.

"We are therefore calling on all Christians to be law abiding but defend themselves whenever the need arises."

An unidentified woman, centre, who lost her husband mourns during a mass funeral of those killed in a Christmas Day bombing at a Catholic church in Madalla, Nigeria. The Pentagon's Joint Improvised Explosive Device Defeat Organization (JIEDDO) says that bomb attacks in Nigeria, Kenya and Somalia became more frequent and deadly in 2011 as al-Qaida-affiliated terror groups used more sophisticated devices to kill more people with each explosion, February 1, 2011. (AP Photo/Sunday Aghaeze, File)

Kabiru Sokoto, who police accuse of masterminding the Christmas Day bombing of St. Theresa Catholic church appears before journalists during a news conference at the headquarters of the State Security Service in Abuja, February 10, 2012. (AP Photo/Sunday Aghaeze)

4

Human Rights

Nigeria's President Goodluck Jonathan addresses the United Nations General Assembly, at U.N. headquarters. Former Nigeria President Olusegun Obasanjo has openly accused Nigeria's President Goodluck Jonathan of corruption and that he is training a death squad to kill his enemies, but Jonathan has challenged the allegations in a letter posted on his special adviser's website Monday December 23, 2013. Jonathan said he has asked security agencies and the government-funded National Commission for Human Rights to investigate Obasanjo's suggestion that he is training a killer squad to assassinate some of the 1,000-plus enemies on a hit list, September 24, 2013. (AP Photo/Richard Drew, FILE)

Nigerian President Declares State of Emergency
December 31, 2011
By Bashir Adigun

Nigeria's president on Saturday (December 31) declared a state of emergency in parts of Africa's most populous nation, after a recent slew of deadly attacks blamed on a northern-based radical Muslim sect killed dozens of people, as separate communal clashes in the country's southeast left more than 40 dead.

President Goodluck Jonathan declared an indefinite state of emergency in four states, which would all allow security agencies there to make arrests without proof and conduct searches without warrants. He also ordered the closure of international borders near the affected areas.

They include parts of northeastern state of Yobe and the central states of Plateau and Niger, all hit by the Christmas Day attacks that left at least 42 people dead, for which a radical sect known as Boko Haram claimed responsibility. Attackers targeted churches and one of the state offices of Nigeria's secret police.

The president also declared a state of emergency in parts of the northeastern state of Borno, a stronghold of the feared Islamic sect.

"What began as sectarian crises in the northeastern parts of the country has gradually evolved into terrorist activities in different parts of the country with attendant negative consequences on our national security," Jonathan said.

"(The state of emergency) means extra powers to security agencies in those areas," said National Security Adviser Owoye Azazi, who also told journalists in Abuja that it would last "until the situation improves."

Jonathan also said Saturday that he has directed top security officials to set up a special counterterrorism unit to fight the growing threat posed by Boko Haram.

Earlier in the year, an Aug. 26 bombing of the United Nations headquarters in Nigeria's capital Abuja killed 24 people and wounded 116 others. The sect claimed responsibility for that attack.

The Christmas attacks come a year after a series of Christmas Eve bombings in central city of Jos in the nation's "middle belt," where the country's largely Muslim north meets its largely Christian south. Last year's Christmas attacks claimed by the militants left at least 32 dead and 74 wounded.

"Terrorism is a war against all of us," Jonathan said as he spoke during an address on national television on Saturday. "I call on all Nigerians to join hands with government to fight these terrorists."

The sect, some of whose members are believed to have links to al-Qaida, wants to impose Islamic Shariah law across Nigeria.

The U.S. Embassy had warned U.S. citizens late Friday to exercise caution in Nigeria.

"Violent extremist attacks have continued in various locations, including the states of Bauchi, Borno, Gombe, Kaduna, Kano, Niger, Plateau, and Yobe, resulting in numerous casualties," the warning read.

Boko Haram's widening terror attacks, though, are only further intensifying religious and ethnic divisions in Nigeria. In this nation of more than 160 million people, thousands have died in recent years in communal fighting pitting machete-wielding neighbors against each other.

Bodies of people alleged to have been killed in an attack on a town hall meeting of the Christian Igbo ethnic group lie on the floor in a hospital morgue in Mubi, in the Adamawa state of northern Nigeria, Saturday. The town hall attack, which left at least 20 dead, is one of a string of deadly attacks claimed by Boko Haram, which has promised to kill Christians living in Nigeria's largely Muslim north, January 7, 2012. (AP Photo)

In the southeastern state of Ebonyi, more than 40 people died in clashes early Saturday morning between the Ezza and Ezillo peoples who have long-standing rivalries, said state police spokesman John Elu. He said troops had been deployed, but the situation was still tense.

The conflict, which occurred far from the regions affected by the state of emergency, has no apparent link to the Islamic insurgency that has erupted in mostly northern states. However, such clashes add to Nigeria's serious security concerns which Boko Haram has exacerbated over the last year.

The sect came to national prominence in 2009, when its members rioted and burned police stations near its base of Maiduguri, a dusty northeastern city on the cusp of the Sahara Desert. Nigeria's military violently put down the attack, crushing the sect's mosque into shards as its leader was arrested and died in police custody. About 700 people died during the violence.

While initially targeting enemies via hit-and-run assassinations from the back of motorbikes after the 2009 riot, violence by Boko Haram now has a new sophistication and apparent planning that includes high-profile attacks with greater casualties. That has fueled speculation about the group's ties as it has splintered into at least three different factions, diplomats and security sources say. They say the more extreme wing of the sect maintains contact with terror groups in North Africa and Somalia.

Targeting the group has remained difficult, as sect members are scattered throughout northern Nigeria and nearby Cameroon, Chad and Niger.

Kano Assault Most Deadly Yet
January 22, 2012
By Jon Gambrell

People in this north Nigeria city once wore surgical masks to block the dust swirling through its sprawling neighborhoods, but swarming children hawked the masks for pennies apiece Sunday (January 22) to block the stench of death at a hospital overflowing with the dead following a coordinated attack by a radical Islamist sect.

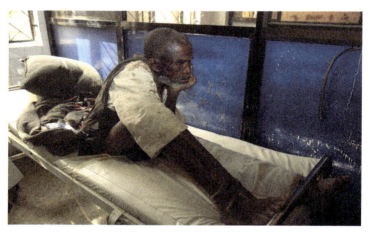

An unidentified victim of the January 20 suicide bombing receives treatment at the accident and emergency unit Murtala Mohammed specialist hospital, in Kano following recent sectarian attacks. The emir of Kano and the state's top politician offered prayers for the more than 150 people who were killed in a coordinated series of attacks by Boko Haram, January 23, 2012. (AP Photo/Sunday Alamba)

The Nigerian Red Cross now estimates more than 150 people died in Friday's attack in Kano, which saw at least two suicide bombers from the sect known as Boko Haram detonate explosive-laden cars. The scope of the attack, apparently planned to free sect members held by authorities here, left even President Goodluck Jonathan speechless as he toured what remained of a regional police headquarters Sunday.

"The federal government will not rest until we arrest the perpetrators of this act," Jonathan said earlier. "They are not spirits, they are not ghosts.

Ado Bayaro, the Emir of Kano, is seen at his palace in Kano. A witness and official say that gunmen attacked the convoy of Ado Bayaro a religious leader in Nigeria's northwest, killing at least three people, January 23, 2012. (AP Photo/ Sunday Alamba, file)

However, unrest continued across Nigeria as unknown assailants in the northern state of Bauchi killed at least 11 people overnight Saturday in attacks that saw at least two churches bombed, a sign how far insecurity has penetrated Africa's most populous nation.

Friday's attacks by Boko Haram hit police stations, immigration offices and the local headquarters of Nigeria's secret police in Kano, a city of more than 9 million people that remains an important political and religious center in the country's Muslim north. The assault left corpses lying in the streets across the city, many wearing police or other security agency uniforms.

On Sunday, soldiers wearing bulky bulletproof vests stood guard at intersections and roundabouts, with bayoneted Kalashnikov rifles at the ready. Some made those disobeying traffic directions do sit-ups or in one case, repeatedly raise a bicycle over their head.

Signs of the carnage still remained. Police officers wearing surgical masks escorted a corpse wrapped in a white burial shroud out of Murtala Muhammed Specialist Hospital, the city's biggest. Hospital officials there declined to comment Sunday, but the smell of the overflowing mortuary hung in the air.

An internal Red Cross report seen Sunday by an Associated Press reporter said that hospital alone has accepted more than 150 dead bodies from the attacks. That death toll could rise further as officials continue to collect bodies.

At least four foreigners were wounded in the attack, the report showed. Among the dead was Indian citizen Kevalkumar Rajput, 23, the Press Trust of India news agency reported.

A man push his bicycle walks past the ruins of a market outside the state police headquarters in Kano. Police said that members of Boko Haram dressed in uniforms resembling those of soldiers and police officers when they launched their attack. At least 185 people died in the attacks, January 24, 2012. (AP Photo/Sunday Alamba)

Jonathan arrived to the city late Sunday afternoon, traveling quickly by a motorcade to meet with the state governor and the Emir of Kano, an important Islamic figure in the country. His motorcade later rushed to what used to be the regional command headquarters for the Nigeria police, with an armed personnel carrier trailing behind, a soldier manning the heavy machine gun atop it.

The Christian president, wearing a Muslim prayer cap and a black kaftan, looked stunned as he stood near where the suicide car bomber detonated his explosives. Officers there said guards on duty shot the tires of the speeding car, forcing it to stop before it reached the lobby of the headquarters.

However, it didn't matter in the end as the powerful explosives in the car shredded the cement building, tore away its roof and blew out its windows. Blood stained the yellow paint near a second-story window, just underneath a 10-foot-tall tree uprooted and tossed atop the building by the blast.

"Whether you are a policeman or not a policeman, when you see this kind of thing, definitely you'll be worried," said Aminu Ringim, a senior police officer. "You'll be touched."

U.N. Secretary-General Ban Ki-moon also condemned the multiple attacks Sunday.

An unidentified victim of the January 20 suicide bombing is been transferred to a ward at the Murtala Mohammed specialist hospital, in Kano, January 23, 2012. (AP Photo/Sunday Alamba)

"The secretary-general is appalled at the frequency and intensity of recent attacks in Nigeria, which demonstrate a wanton and unacceptable disregard for human life," a statement from his office read. He also expressed "his hope for swift and transparent investigations into these incidents that lead to bringing the perpetrators to justice."

A Boko Haram spokesman using the nom de guerre Abul-Qaqa claimed responsibility for the attacks in a message to journalists Friday. He said the attack came because the state government refused to release Boko Haram members held by the police.

The coordinated attack in Kano represents Boko Haram's deadliest assault since beginning a campaign of terror last year that saw a suicide bomber strike the United Nations headquarters in Abuja and at least 510 people killed by the sect, according to an AP count.

So far this year, the group has been blamed for 226 killings, according to an AP count.

Nigeria's weak central government repeatedly has been unable to stop attacks by Boko Haram, whose name means "Western education is sacrilege" in the Hausa language of Nigeria's north.

The group has carried out increasingly sophisticated and bloody attacks in its campaign to implement strict Shariah law and avenge the deaths of Muslims in communal violence across Nigeria, a multiethnic nation of more than 160 million people split largely into a Christian south and Muslim north.

While the sect has begun targeting Christian living in the north, the majority of those killed Friday appeared to be Muslim, officials have said.

Violence continued Sunday in Nigeria's north. In Bauchi state, local police commissioner Ikechukwu Aduba said at least 11 people were killed in assaults there that also saw two churches attacked.

It was unclear what started the violence, though communal violence remains occurs between the area's different ethnic groups. Bauchi, about 200 miles from Kano, is also a region where Boko Haram has staged attacks before.

Human Rights Violations
January 24, 2012
By Jon Gambrell

A young man in traditional robes sobbed Tuesday (January 24) as he stood in a pool of blood, surrounded by bullet-scarred walls left behind after a security raid in this northern Nigeria city recently assaulted by a radical Islamist sect.

Residents of this dusty neighborhood in the city of Kano pressed shoulder-to-shoulder inside the home, saying soldiers and others killed the man who lived here and his pregnant wife for no reason.

Ibrahim Idris, Kano state police commissioner, speaks to journalists in his office in Kano, January 24, 2012. (AP Photo/Sunday Alamba)

The local police commissioner acknowledged the attack and said it was part of the government's effort to root out the sect known as Boko Haram, responsible for killing at least 185 people in a Friday attack on the country's second-largest city.

Tuesday's killings highlight the dangers posed by possible reprisal killings and arbitrary arrests carried out by Nigerian security services who are trying to stop Boko Haram's increasingly sophisticated attacks. And while the sect remains amorphous and secretive, such assaults may only alienate the same population the government wants to save.

"He didn't belong to any religious group. Is it because of his beard?" asked relative Musa Ibrahim Fatega. "That means you cannot dress the way you are. Is it good? Is this how government is going to treat us?"

Friday's attack in Kano saw Boko Haram members spread through the city, attacking police stations, immigration offices and the local headquarters of the secret police. The attacks came after authorities refused to release suspected sect members earlier arrested, Kano state police commissioner Ibrahim Idris said.

Much of the bloodshed during Friday's attack occurred when Boko Haram gunmen threw improvised bombs made of aluminum cans and a white powder explosive, likely fertilizer. Foreign journalists saw the cans Tuesday, which had been stuffed with cotton at the top, each holding a simple detonator. Idris said gunmen threw the explosives, then fired randomly on those they saw fleeing the blast.

A police officer collects undetonated explosives recovered from Islamic militants in Kano, January 24, 2012. (AP Photo/Sunday Alamba)

Police say they found 10 car bombs and about 300 of those unexploded cans after the attack potentially signaling Boko Haram planned further violence in the city of more than 9 million people.

Some Boko Haram gunmen also wore uniforms resembling those of the Mobile Police, the paramilitary arm of the nation's federal police, to take control of the streets during Friday's attack, Idris said. Others had camouflage uniforms like those worn by soldiers in the country, the commissioner said.

"Some of our police officers who saw them on the street thought they were their colleagues," Idris said. "They just shot them in cold blood."

The coordinated attack was Boko Haram's deadliest since they began a campaign of terror last year. Boko Haram has now killed at least 262 people in 2012, more than half of the at least 510 people the sect killed in all of 2011, according to an Associated Press count. Medical workers and emergency officials say they expect the toll may be even higher.

Boko Haram wants to implement strict Shariah law and avenge the deaths of Muslims in communal violence across Nigeria, a multiethnic nation of more than 160 million people split largely into a Christian south and Muslim north.

While the sect has begun targeting Christians in the north, the majority of those killed Friday appeared to be Muslim, officials said.

Nigeria's weak central government has been unable to stop Boko Haram's increasingly bloody attacks. Early Tuesday morning, security forces surrounded the Kano home and started a gun battle that lasted for hours. It left bullet holes peppering walls and the home's interior metal doors. Inside a living room, blood pooled around beige sofas, with a single rifle cartridge left behind.

Soldiers gather around the body of a suspected Boko Haram sect member after he was shot by soldiers in Maiduguri. The man was killed after trying to shoot at the soldiers while driving a taxi colored car, used in evading security personnel at checkpoints. Near him is an automatic rifle and a full magazine, February 29, 2012. (AP Photo/Abdulkareem Haruna)

A sedan inside the compound, also riddled with bullet holes, bore federal government license plates. The dead man previously worked for the country's education ministry, said Fatega, his relative.

Security forces took the two bodies away, leaving family members to try to figure out how to reclaim them for burial before sundown according to Islamic tradition. The scene around the house was tense as onlookers pressed against the front gate. A military attack helicopter circled overhead.

Idris said a "sister agency" carried out the attack on the house. Typically, police use that term when referring to the State Security Service, the county's secret police. Marilyn Ogar, a secret police spokeswoman, said she had no information about the attack.

Meanwhile, officers have withdrawn from Kano's streets, massing at the state headquarters where one Boko Haram suicide bomber detonated a car full of explosives Friday. Those there remain angry and tense, with one claiming he hadn't eaten for days. Coupled with a military which has used its firepower against civilians in the past, that raises the possibility of innocent people being caught up in security operations or killed, analysts warn.

Suspected members of the Abu Mohammed-led faction of the radical Islamic sect Boko Haram, Bashir Ibrhim, left, Ibrahim Habibu, center, and Gambo Maiborodi, are presented to the media while awaiting official charges for alleged involvement in the kidnap and killing of an Italian and a British national, at the headquarters of the State Security Service headquarters in Nigeria's capital Abuja Nigeria. The Briton and Italian kidnapped in Nigeria were abducted by a splinter cell of a radical Islamist sect and executed before a failed commando rescue operation, the nation's secret police said, March 14, 2012. (AP Photos/Gbemiga Olamikan)

Amnesty International issued a statement Tuesday warning the Nigerian government "not pursue security at the expense of human rights."

"The population in northern Nigeria are caught between being targeted by Boko Haram and Nigeria's counterterrorism measures that fail to prevent, investigate, prosecute or punish these acts," Amnesty said. Such government operations "often result in new human rights violations perpetrated by the security forces with impunity."

However, the situation remains much simpler for police.

"People attacking police stations, they are terrorists," Idris said. "That's it."

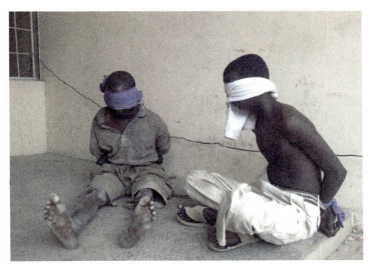

Suspected members of Boko Haram are detained by the military, in Bukavu Barracks in Kano state, Nigeria after an attack on a police headquarters, the home of a senior police officer and setting fire to a nearby bank. Now, Boko Haram seems to be growing ever-stronger, killing more people than ever before and slowly internationalizing their outlook, a possible danger for the rest of West Africa. More than 770 people have been killed in Boko Haram attacks so far this year, according to an Associated Press count, making 2012 the worst year of violence attributed to the group, March 21, 2012. (AP Photos/Salisu Rabiu-file)

Government Pressure on Human Rights Leader
April 16, 2012
By Jon Gambrell

Nigeria's federal police want to interrogate the leader of the nation's human rights commission over comments he made about officers carrying out so-called "extrajudicial" killings in the country, a practice widely documented by activists, his lawyer said Monday (April 16).

Activists in Nigeria warn the demand to question Chidi Anselm Odinkalu could have a chilling effect in Nigeria, a young democracy where authorities still use security agencies to suppress dissent.

Odinkalu, the chairman of the National Human Rights Commission, received a written request from investigators at police headquarters in

Nigeria's capital Abuja to appear for questioning, lawyer Bamidele Aturu said. The request comes from a talk Odinkalu gave March 5 in which he said that the police force "executes well over 2,500 detainees summarily every year," Aturu said.

Police had asked Odinkalu to appear Monday, but Aturu said the human rights commission chairman had a medical appointment previously scheduled. Aturu said he and others had been trying to reach police to reschedule the interrogation, but had been unable to reach the officers involved.

Chidi Anselm Odinkalu, chairman of the National Human Rights Commission speaks during an interview in Lagos, March 24, 2014. (AP Photo/Sunday Alamba)

"There is no way he would honor the appointment at the expense and at the risk of his health," Aturu said Monday.

Olusola Amore, a federal police spokesman, said Monday that he had no information about the interrogation request and declined to comment.

The killing of arrestees by police officers in Nigeria remains an open secret in this country of more than 160 million people. Studies by Amnesty International and Human Rights Watch have repeatedly documented cases of underpaid and undertrained officers killing suspects with impunity. The police use euphemisms for the slayings, saying the suspects would be "escorted," sent out on an "errand" or "transferred to" Nigeria's capital Abuja, the reports claim.

Mohammed D. Abubakar, who took over as police inspector general in January, gave a speech in February in which he said that "justice has been perverted, people's rights denied, innocent souls committed to prison, torture and extra-judicial killings perpetrated."

It's unclear why police now want to speak with Odinkalu, who heads the federal human rights agency. In a statement, Amnesty International condemned what it described as the "police intimidation" Odinkalu faces.

The bodies of three alleged Boko Haram sect members who attacked security forces, at a check point in Kano. Lt. Iweha Ikedichi, joint task force spokesperson, told journalists during a briefing at Bukavu barracks in Kano that the three were killed after they stole a car at gun point, April 4, 2012. (AP Photo/Salisu Rabiu)

"The police ought to be spending their time and energy investigating allegations of extrajudicial executions, enforced disappearances and torture committed by their officers, rather than harassing the National Human Rights Commission," said Erwin van der Borght, Amnesty's Africa director.

More Extrajudicial Killings
October 8, 2012
By Haruna Umar

Nigerian soldiers angry about the killing of an officer shot dead more than 30 civilians Monday (October 8) in a northeastern city long under siege by a radical Islamist sect.

The attack came from soldiers attached to a special military unit on guard in Maiduguri, the spiritual home of the sect known as Boko Haram, in an effort to supposedly protect its citizens from the violence gripping the city. The killings likely will further antagonize a population already alienated by checkpoints, security force harassment and the threat of being killed by soldiers who are targets for the sect's increasingly bloody guerrilla attacks.

In this frame from TV footage shot by the Nigeria television authority shows people lying down (condition of people unknown) on a street in Maiduguri. Nigerian officials dumped dozens of corpses in front of a hospital in northeast Nigeria after soldiers opened fire and killed more than 30 civilians. The hospital, overwhelmed by the scale of the violence, had to turn away the dead as its morgue had no more room. The killings come as besieged, underpaid and enraged soldiers remain targets of guerrilla attacks by Boko Haram, October 8, 2012. (AP Photo / Nigeria Television Authority)

An Associated Press reporter in Maiduguri counted the dead while on a tour of the still-smoldering neighborhood Monday afternoon. The journalist saw no weapons or evidence that the dead belonged to the sect. A soldier nearby, who did not identify himself, claimed the attack was a response to a bombing nearby earlier Monday that he said killed a lieutenant.

"They killed our officer!" the soldier shouted. "We had no options!"

The AP reporter also saw that soldiers had set fire to about 50 homes and businesses around the area, which sits near the Nigerian Union of Journalists state office and other buildings in Maiduguri. It appeared the soldiers attacked the area using assault rifles and heavy machine guns mounted on armored personnel carriers. Rounds shot from the heavy machine guns destroyed cars and set roofs on fire, which razed buildings and caused damage at a two-story shopping complex.

The journalist accompanied Zanna Umar Mustapha, the deputy governor of Borno state, on the tour.

State officials declined to comment about the killings and urged those traveling with the convoy not to take photographs of the destruction out of fear of further alienating those living in the region.

Soldiers walk past burnt out houses in Maiduguri, October 8, 2012. (AP Photo / Nigeria Television Authority)

Nigeria's military has been accused of committing so-called "extrajudicial killings" while in pursuit of the Boko Haram sect. The military now routinely claims massive operations with dozens of people killed, always referred to as Boko Haram members or sympathizers, announcements that cannot be independently verified. The military also downplays its own casualties suffered during the operations.

Lt. Col. Sagir Musa, a spokesman for the military force in the city, declined to immediately comment about the retaliatory attack. Earlier in the day, he had said that two soldiers were wounded in the bombing. Col. Mohammed Yerima, a military spokesman in Nigeria's capital, Abuja, did not immediately respond to a request for comment Monday night.

The killing of civilians comes as Boko Haram continues its bloody guerrilla campaign against Nigeria's weak central government. The sect, whose name means "Western education is sacrilege" in the Hausa language of Nigeria's north, is blamed for killing more than 690 people in drive-by killings and bombings this year alone, according to an AP count. The sect has demanded the release of all its captive members and has called for strict Shariah law to be implemented across the entire country.

The sect has killed both Christians and Muslims in their attacks, as well as soldiers and security forces. Nigeria's military has claimed it has killed a number of the sect's senior leadership in recent days, including operational commanders and the sect's spokesman, who used the nom de guerre Abul Qaqa. However, the sect's leader, Abubakar Shekau, has eluded capture and continues to make Internet videos that taunt and threaten further violence against Nigerian government officials and security forces.

Diplomats and Western security officials say Boko Haram has loose links to African terror groups, al-Qaida in the Islamic Maghreb and al-Shabab of Somalia.

The killing of members of the sect's senior leadership comes as the group recently changed some of its tactics and attacked more than 30 mobile phone towers throughout northern Nigeria, disrupting communications in a nation reliant on cellular phones.

Meanwhile, authorities blamed the sect for the shooting death Sunday of a Chinese national in a town outside of Maiduguri.

Human Rights Watch Report
October 11, 2012
By Jon Gambrell

Nigerian security forces and the radical Islamist Boko Haram sect likely committed crimes against humanity in their fighting across the country's Muslim north, both torturing and killing civilians as bloodshed in the region grows, according to a report released Thursday (October 11).

The Human Rights Watch report comes just days after soldiers angered by the killing of an officer shot dead more than 30 civilians with machine guns and burned down buildings in a neighborhood in Maiduguri, the spiritual home of Boko Haram.

The report calls on the International Criminal Court to examine the actions of all sides in the conflict and to push for prosecutions of those involved, though it stops short of calling for international proceedings against those involved.

"All parties should respect international human rights standards and halt the downward spiral of violence that terrorizes residents in northern and central Nigeria," states the report.

Boko Haram, whose name means "Western education is sacrilege" in the Hausa language of Nigeria's north, is blamed for killing more than 690 people in drive-by killings and bombings this year alone, according to an Associated Press count. The sect has demanded the release of all its captive members and has called for strict Shariah law to be implemented across the entire country.

Chidi Anselm Odinkalu, chairman of the National Human Rights Commission speaks during an interview in Lagos, Nigeria. Two generals and officials of Nigeria's feared State Security Service had to testify under oath at a hearing of the National Human Rights Commission into killings of unarmed civilians — a "quantum leap" in accountability in Nigeria, according to the country's top rights advocate. The December hearings were the first time such high-ranking officers, including the chief of army staff, have been held to account since Nigeria's military dictatorship, said Chidi Anselm Odinkalu, chairman of the National Human Rights Commission. It published a report blaming State Security agents for the unlawful gunning down of eight civilians and wounding of 11 others, and ordered the government to pay reparations of some $820,000, March 24, 2014. (AP Photo/Sunday Alamba)

The sect has killed both Christians and Muslims in their attacks, as well as soldiers and security forces. Despite leaders enacting martial law and sending more troops into the region, the sect's attacks continue almost unstopped. Recently, the military claimed it killed a number of the sect's senior leaders, as well as put out statements claiming to have killed dozens of other members in its operations.

However, a bombing Monday morning by suspected Boko Haram members, that a soldier said killed a lieutenant, sparked a violent retaliation by the army in Maiduguri, the sect's spiritual home. Troops opened fire with assault rifles and heavy machine guns mounted on armored personnel carriers on a busy street near the local headquarters of the Nigerian Union of Journalists, according to witnesses. Afterward, an AP journalist counted the bodies more than 30 dead civilians and saw more than 50 shops and homes burned.

The military later denied it killed civilians, but offered contradictory explanations about what happened. Activists say they worry that other military strikes against Boko Haram may have killed civilians as well.

The Human Rights Watch report also alleges the military, as well as the police, have used torture and indefinite detentions against the civilian population. One witness who spoke to the group said he saw soldiers torture an inmate at a Maiduguri barracks by "pulling on his genitals with a pair of pliers," while another peeled the skin of a detainee with a razor. The witness said soldiers killed another detainee as he hung from a tree.

The report also claimed the police and military routinely kill and extort civilians. The military denied the allegations, with the report quoting officials as saying that they didn't hold prisoners at the barracks and that "there is no Guantanamo Bay" in Nigeria.

"Despite allegations of widespread security force abuses, the Nigerian authorities have rarely held anyone accountable, thereby denying justice to the victims and further solidifying the culture of impunity for violence in Nigeria," the report reads. "Government officials often issue blanket denials of reports of alleged human rights violations and almost never give a public account, in the communities they are meant to serve, of the measures taken to investigate reports of abuses."

The report also went into details about the violence used by Boko Haram, including killing Christians who refused to convert to Islam. One man recounted how in 2009 a preacher continued to preach while being held by Boko Haram members, saying those held "should not betray Jesus."

"They beat him and then carried him away," the man recounted. "I saw one of them cut the back of his neck with a sword. He didn't die right away but continued to struggle."

The Boko Haram violence at times appears aimed at triggering more ethnic and religious violence in Nigeria, a nation largely split between a predominantly Muslim north and a Christian south. Attacks have targeted churches in central Nigeria, where mass killings have occurred before.

"It is a strategy by Boko Haram to bring the government to its knees by creating a war situation," a Nigerian journalist said, according to the report.

Soldiers stand guard outside St. Rita's Catholic church in Kaduna, Nigeria. A suicide bomber rammed an SUV loaded with explosives into the church holding Mass on Sunday killing at least seven people and wounding more than 100 others in an attack that sparked reprisal killings in the city, October 28, 2012. (AP Photo)

5

Spilling Over Borders

A soldier inspects the bridge that links Nigeria and Cameroon following an attacked by Islamic militants in Gambaru, Nigeria. Thousands of members of Boko Haram strike across the border in Cameroon, with coordinated attacks on border towns. Further north, Boko Haram employs recruits from Chad to enforce its control in northeastern Nigerian towns and cities. In Niger, the government has declared a "humanitarian crisis" and appealed for international aid to help tens of thousands of Nigerian refugees driven from their homes by the insurgency, May 11, 2014. (AP Photo/Jossy Ola, File)

French Hostages from Cameroon
April 19, 2013
By Divine Ntaryike and Lori Hinnant

A French family with four young children kidnapped at gunpoint by Islamic extremists in northern Cameroon was freed after two months of captivity in what the father described as especially harsh conditions following the group's return Friday (April 19) to safety in the Cameroonian capital.

Cameroonian television showed the family of seven four children, their parents and their uncle stepping off an airplane, a man who had grown a thick beard carrying the smallest child. All appeared thin, but walked steadily.

Officials from France and Cameroon offered no details on how the family was freed overnight, and it was not clear whether there were concessions to the kidnappers.

Tanguy Moulin-Fournier, an expatriate employee for a French company and father of the family, said in a brief radio interview that the group learned their release was imminent just a few hours beforehand and that their return to safety went well.

Speaking hours later at the ambassador's residence of the French Embassy in Yaounde, Cameroon's capital, he said the group has to "digest" their freedom before responding to questions while still "in the grip of emotions."

"It was very difficult," Moulin-Fournier, now sporting a thick beard, said. "It's the end of the dry season. The heat is terrible. Water was a problem. It was difficult to hold out."

The children, who the French media reported were aged 5 to 12, fared better, he said.

"Children have something in them so that they manage to hold up," he said. "Life in them flows stronger."

The seven ex-hostages were freed "in a zone between Nigeria and Cameroon," Foreign Minister Laurent Fabius said.

"It's a day of happiness, extraordinary happiness, for all French people to know that the Moulin-Fournier family is finally free, safe and sound," he said late Friday in a ceremony held in the Cameroonian capital before he was due to escort the family back to France.

"All hostage-takings are strongly felt in France, but this one was perhaps felt more because it concerned a big family with little kids."

French President Francois Hollande said authorities made contact with the kidnappers through intermediaries, and negotiations intensified in recent days. He reiterated France's official policy against ransom payments.

"We use all our contacts, but remain firm on our principles," Hollande said. "We are not changing the principle that France does not pay ransoms."

France has come under criticism over what diplomats and analysts say is an unofficial policy of indirectly paying ransoms through middlemen over the years. Vicki Huddleston, a former U.S. ambassador to Mali, alleged that

France paid a $17 million ransom to free hostages seized from a French mining site cash she said ultimately funded the al-Qaida-linked militants in Mali. French officials deny paying any ransoms.

French President Francois Hollande, left, delivers a speech to welcome former hostages Tanguy Moulin-Fournier, center, and his brother Cyril Moulin-Fournier, second from right, arriving from Yaounde, at the Orly airport near Paris. The French members of the Moulin-Fournier family were released after being held in Nigeria for two months by Boko Haram and left Cameroon for France on April 19, 2013 accompanied by French Foreign Minister Laurent Fabius, April 20, 2013. (AP Photo/Thomas Samson, Pool)

Fabius, like Hollande, stressed the need for discretion in working to free hostages. The minister thanked Cameroonian President Paul Biya and the Nigerian head of state.

"The Cameroonian people and I are filled with great relief and great joy to see you free," Biya told the three freed adults who attended a ceremony in the capital late Friday.

The Feb. 19 kidnapping in northern Cameroon near the Nigerian border came as thousands of French troops were deeply involved in a military intervention against Islamic extremists in the west African country of Mali. The French statement recalled that eight other French citizens are still being held hostage in the Sahel region of Africa.

Moulin-Fournier is an employee of the French gas group GDF Suez and worked in Yaounde.

"We were not involved in any negotiations but we knew that French authorities were very active," Gerard Mastrallet, the head of GDF, said in an interview with RTL radio.

Last month, a video surfaced showing a man who appeared to be Moulin-Fournier. The man said his family was in the custody of the Islamic radical sect known as Boko Haram which wants all its members freed, especially women and children held in Nigerian and Cameroonian custody.

Boko Haram has been waging a campaign of bombings and shootings across Nigeria's north. They are held responsible for more than 790 deaths last year, and dozens more since the beginning of this year.

Moulin-Fournier had said his family was not doing well in captivity.

"We lose force (strength) every day and start to be sick; we will not stay very long like this," he said in the recording.

Neither Nigeria nor Cameroon reported any Boko Haram members were freed.

Brig. Gen. Chris Olukolade, a Nigerian defense ministry spokesman, told The Associated Press on Friday that the release followed a "meticulous collaboration between the Nigerian security forces and French counterparts, as well as others." However, he declined to offer any other information.

"I can only inform you that we collaborated," he said.

Nigerian presidential spokesman Reuben Abati and a spokeswoman for Nigeria's domestic spy agency also declined to comment. However, it appeared Nigerian authorities were caught off-guard by the announcement.

Vigilantes Target Boko Haram
June 12, 2013
By Haruna Umar

Young men armed with machetes and sticks have entered the streets of Nigeria's biggest city in the northeast to target suspected Islamic extremists, even as soldiers continued an offensive against the radical fighters.

The vigilante group, known as "Civilian JTF," a play off the acronym used to describe the joint military and police taskforce in the region, started taking up arms after President Goodluck Jonathan declared a state of emergency May 14 in Adamawa, Borno and Yobe states a territory of around 155,000 square kilometers (60,000 square miles) of the Sahel bordering Cameroon, Chad and Niger.

Vigilantes of the civilian JTF with cutlasses and clubs mount a check point on the street of Maiduguridamaturu, August 7, 2013. (AP Photo/Sunday Alamba)

Nigeria security forces, left, watch as a member of the "Civilian JTF" right, pushes a man during an event, in Maiduguri. They are part of a vigilante force that has arisen here as a backlash against Boko Haram, August 8, 2013. (AP Photo/Sunday Alamba)

In a nationally televised speech, Jonathan admitted the nation had lost control of some villages and towns to extremist fighters already responsible for more than 1,600 killings since 2010 alone, according to an Associated Press count.

In the time since, the military claims it has killed and arrested suspected extremists as it now controls security for the region with expanded powers to arrest anyone and occupy any building. However, military officials who spoke to journalists on a recent trip through the northeast acknowledged many fighters likely fled with heavy weaponry including anti-aircraft guns and still remain a major threat to Africa's most populous nation.

The members of Civilian JTF have now come under attack from extremists for pointing out suspects to soldiers.

Borno state governor, Kashim Shettima, right, shakes hands with members of the "Civilian JTF" during an event in Maiduguri. Thousands of suspected members of Boko Haram arrested in Maiduguri, birthplace of the Islamic extremist terrorist network, have been discovered by these young volunteers who call themselves the "Civilian JTF," fashioned after the military Joint Task Force sent to enforce a 3-month-old state of emergency and hunt the extremists down, August 8, 2013. (AP Photo/Sunday Alamba)

An AP reporter met a group of the young men belonging to the vigilantes recently in the streets of Maiduguri, the capital of Borno state and the spiritual home of the extremist network Boko Haram. The men ranged in age from 17 to 25 and carried machetes, iron bars and batons to protect themselves.

The men said they formed their own patrols after becoming tired of soldiers routinely rounding up any young man found in a neighborhood after an extremist attack in the city. Soldiers in Nigeria's military, drawn from across the more than 250 ethnicities in the nation, can have difficulties speaking local languages and understanding customs in regions far from their home. The young men said their local knowledge helps the soldiers do their job better.

"We are into this to salvage our people from the Boko Haram who had killed our people, security operatives and destroyed our economy," vigilante Isa Musa said. "We are not afraid of them because we are doing a just cause and God is by our side."

Musa said the vigilantes didn't fear the extremists, even though their fighters carry Kalashnikov assault rifles and other sophisticated weaponry.

"All we want is prayers from the people and their cooperation. We are working together with the JTF soldiers," he said. "We want government to assist us with more weapons like cutlasses, iron batons and axes."

Last Friday, however, the Civilian JTF members found themselves a target of a suspected Boko Haram attack. Gunmen hid their assault rifles inside a coffin and opened fire on them in Maiduguri. At least 13 people were killed in that attack, witnesses said.

It's not clear whether these civilian groups receive either the passive acceptance or the endorsement of the military now securing Maiduguri, though it would appear likely as soldiers seem to allow their movement in a city filled with sandbagged roadblocks. Lt. Col. Sagir Musa, a military spokesman in the city, could not be reached for comment as security forces have shut down mobile phone networks in the northeast as part of the offensive.

What is known is that suspects recently pointed out by the vigilantes in three cases ended up dead. Two were shot and killed for "trying to escape," a witness recently said. An AP journalist saw the bodies of eight other suspected extremists dead in a ditch after being pointed out last week by vigilantes. Human rights activists and international organizations routinely document cases of soldiers and police carrying out so-called "extrajudicial killings" in Nigeria, meaning that those pointed out could end up dead or imprisoned without charges.

However, those concerns don't bother the civilians, who continue their armed patrols.

"We have lost count of how many Boko Haram we have caught and handed over to the soldiers," vigilante Abubakar Malum said. "And we are going after more of them."

Refugees Flee to Cameroon
July 3, 2013
By Haruna Umar

At least 20,000 refugees have fled to Cameroon from northeast Nigerian villages that have become hideouts for Islamic militants, a Nigerian lawmaker said.

A community leader said people also fled attacks by the Nigerian military a charge in line with reports by human rights groups that security forces sent to fight the militants are indiscriminately killing civilians.

Sadiqui Ali said civilians were among 13 suspected extremists killed by the military in two villages in the Gwoza hills on June 15.

Col. Danladi Hassan came to reassure villagers that no soldier would kill anyone unlawfully, he said.

But five days later "we woke up with the sound of gunshots everywhere, which resulted in the killings of 8 persons (civilians)," he charged. Ali was speaking to Nigerian officials who Tuesday visited refugees camped near Ashigashiya town and two other camps in northern Cameroon.

Borno state deputy governor, Zanna Mustapha, listens to a question from a journalist during an exclusive interview in Maiduguri. Using every resource from psychologists to agriculture experts and security forces, the Nigerian state hopes to reach a reservoir of angry and rootless young men easily recruited by Islamic extremists and transform them into productive members of society. "We are trying to look inward at what is the immediate cause and who are these people" in Boko Haram, Mustapha said, August 9, 2013. (AP Photo/Sunday Alamba)

Refugee Suleiman Dalhatu told The Associated Press that he fled because Christians settling scores with Muslims had put his name on a list of suspected extremists given to the military. His claim was vigorously denied by Christians among the refugees.

Religious tensions are rising among refugees and those who remain in northeast Nigeria, where the government declared a state of emergency covering one-sixth of the country last month, admitting militants of the Boko Haram extremist sect had taken control of villages and some towns.

Deputy Gov. Zannah Umar Mustapha of Borno state, where the refugees are from, pleaded with them to return home, saying the government was making necessary arrangements to ensure their safety.

None appeared convinced that the government could protect them. Civilians say they are terrified of both the extremists and the troops sent to put down the insurgency.

Officials have warned of imminent food shortages because farmers have been driven from their fields by the militants or are prevented from reaching them by military roadblocks.

This week, the government announced it has released 25,000 metric tons from the nation's strategic grain reserve to be given to people in the area under a military emergency.

It said the food, comprising more than half a million bags of corn and millet, would be released in batches.

Islamic militants have killed more than 1,600 people since 2010, according to an AP count. Soldiers are accused of killing hundreds more, a charge the military denies.

Hundreds Die in Military Custody
October 15, 2013
By Michelle Faul

Hundreds of people are dying in military detention from shootings, suffocation or starvation as Nigeria's security forces crack down on an Islamic uprising in the northeast, Amnesty International said Tuesday (October 15).

More than 950 people died in military custody in the first six months of this year, according to "credible information" from a senior Nigerian army officer, the rights group said.

The Associated Press reported in August that hundreds of people detained by security forces in northern Nigeria have disappeared. The new Amnesty International report may help explain what happened to all those people a horrifying result for their loved ones who are still searching for the missing.

Military and government officials did not immediately respond to phone calls and emails requesting their comments.

If the number of deaths in military custody cited by the Amnesty International is accurate, that means Nigeria's military has killed more civilians than the extremists did during the first half of 2013.

Amnesty International called for an urgent investigation.

Detainees "were reportedly shot in the leg during interrogations, provided no medical care and left to bleed to death," the London-based human rights group said in the report, which includes testimony from freed detainees.

In this image taken with a mobile phone, rescue workers and family members gather to identify the shrouded bodies of students killed following an attack by Islamist extremists at the Yobe State College of Agriculture in Gujba, Nigeria. Suspected Islamic extremists gunned down students as they slept in dormitories and torched classrooms, leaving some 50 students dead according to college Provost Molima Idi Mato, September 29, 2013. (AP Photo)

The AP reported three months after President Goodluck Jonathan declared a state of emergency in the northeastern states of Adamawa, Borno and Yobe on May 14 that hundreds of people were being rounded up in night raids. The state of emergency gives a Joint Task Force of soldiers, police, intelligence and customs and immigration officials the right to detain people and move them from place to place, as well as the right to search without warrants.

Distraught relatives, human rights organizations and journalists have asked the army, the police, intelligence services and government officials where the arrested people are, but have received no answers, the AP reported.

Amnesty International says dozens of bodies are being delivered by soldiers to the mortuaries of the main hospitals in Maiduguri and Damaturu, capitals of Borno and Yobe states.

Human rights activist Shehu Sani of the northern-based Civil Rights Congress of Nigeria told AP in August that he believes thousands had been detained.

Amnesty International said those killed were detained as suspected members or associates of Boko Haram, an armed Islamic extremist group that has claimed responsibility for attacks that have killed hundreds of Muslim and Christian civilians this year in their mission to overturn democracy and force Nigeria Africa's most populous nation which is almost equally divided between the predominantly Muslim north and mainly Christian south to become an Islamic state.

Boko Haram itself routinely commits human rights abuses, gunning down schoolchildren, health workers, government officials, Christian pastors and moderate Muslim clerics. In 2009, security forces bombed and destroyed the Boko Haram headquarters in Maiduguri. The sect's leader, Mohammed Yusuf, was killed in police custody.

Amnesty International said most of the deaths it documented at the hands of security forces took place at the Presidential Lodge guardroom and a detention center in Damaturu, and at Giwa Military Barracks in Maiduguri.

"The details of what happens behind locked doors in these shadowy detention facilities must be exposed, and those responsible for any human rights violations brought to book," said Amnesty International's deputy Africa director, Lucy Freeman.

Amnesty International quoted a second senior army officer as saying: "Hundreds have been killed in detention either by shooting them or by suffocation. People are crammed into one cell. There are times when people are brought out on a daily basis and killed."

Local and international human rights activists warned when thousands of troops were deployed in May that abuses by the military could help fuel the insurgency.

People inspect the burned down police station following an attack by Boko Haram in Damaturu, October 28, 2013. (AP Photo)

Civilians in northeast Nigeria as well as refugees among more than 30,000 who have fled to Cameroon, Chad and Niger have told AP reporters that they fear Nigeria's military as much as they do Boko Haram.

In April, security forces attacked by Boko Haram at the fishing village of Baga turned their guns on civilians after the militants fled. Witnesses told the AP that 187 civilians were killed by security forces who razed the village.

The military said 37 civilians were killed. There has been no investigation and no repercussions for the perpetrators.

Extremists From Neighboring Countries Joining Up
October 26, 2013
By Michelle Faul

Extremists from three neighboring countries are fighting in Nigeria's northeastern Islamic uprising, according to an alleged captured extremist whose account reinforces fears that one of Africa's most powerful Islamic militant groups is growing closer to al-Qaida affiliates and that radical movements are spilling across national boundaries.

"We do have members from Chad, Niger and Cameroon who actively participate in most of our attacks," said a young man presented to journalists Friday night by Nigeria's military as a captured fighter of the Boko Haram terrorist network.

The claim of foreign fighters indicates the growing influence of Boko Haram, which started out as a machete-wielding gang and that now wages war with armored cars, rocket-propelled grenades and improvised explosive devices in its mission to force all of Nigeria Africa's largest oil producer and a country of 160 million that has almost equal numbers of Christians and Muslims to become an Islamic state.

Boko Haram poses the biggest security threat in years to the cohesion of Nigeria, already riven by sectarian, tribal and regional divisions that often explode into bloodletting, amid power struggles ahead of elections in 2015 that likely will be contested by the current president, a fundamentalist Christian.

A harsh military crackdown in three northeastern states covering one-sixth of the country since mid-May has forced Boko Haram out of major cities and towns, but the security forces appear unable to prevent regular extremist attacks on soft targets like school pupils in which hundreds have been killed in recent months.

President Goodluck Jonathan's government, which is struggling to control the Islamic rebellion, for the first time presented an alleged Boko Haram fighter, a 22-year-old walking on crutches because of a bullet wound suffered when he was captured in a recent attack.

The young man refused to give his name, for fear that his family would be targeted. His account sheds new light on life inside the shadowy Boko Haram, which means "western education is forbidden" in the Hausa language.

The captured extremist member said religion did not figure in his life as a Nigerian Islamic warrior, insisting his leaders "had never once preached Islam to us."

He said the name of Allah was invoked only when "we are running out of food supply in the bush. Our leaders will assemble us and declare that we would be embarking on a mission for God and Islam."

He added: "I did not see any act of religion in there. We are just killing people, stealing and suffering in the bush."

Recently Boko Haram has carried out brutal attacks on mainly Muslim civilians. The new assaults "offer vital and disturbing insights" that "not only confirm many of the group's earlier developments but also al-Qaida in the Islamic Maghreb's, or AQIM's, growing influence over it," Jonathan Hill, senior lecturer at the Defence Studies Department of King's College, London, wrote in an analysis published online.

"These atrocities bear many striking similarities to those carried out by AQIM and its various forbears in Algeria," wrote Hill, who is the author of "Nigeria Since Independence: Forever Fragile?"

He noted that "despite the extraordinary efforts of the security forces, Boko Haram appears unbowed and its campaign undimmed."

Former hostages meet with Cameroonian President, Paul Biya during a reception in Yaounde, Cameroon. Biya received former hostages, 10 Chinese and 17 Cameroonians, who were freed from captivity last week after spending some months held by armed men thought to belong to the militant rebel Islamist group Boko Haram in Nigeria, which has been increasingly making incursions into Cameroon, October 13, 2014. (AP Photo/Fabrice Ngon)

Earlier this week, Justice Minister Mohammed Adoke charged that Boko Haram is being influenced from abroad. "Nigeria is experiencing the impact of externally-induced internal security challenges, manifesting in the activities of militant insurgents," he said while defending the country's record at a meeting of the United Nations Human Rights Council in Geneva.

Adoke did not give any details of the alleged external influences. Boko Haram fighters, including current leader Abubakar Shekau, were reported fighting alongside al-Qaida affiliated groups that seized northern Mali last year. The movement has also boasted that it has fighters trained in Somalia by al-Shabab the group that claimed responsibility for the most spectacular terrorist attack in Africa in recent years that killed at least 67 at Kenya's upscale Westgate Mall last month.

Boko Haram has long been known to be receiving funding from abroad. Founding father Mohammed Yusuf was receiving funds from Iran, Sudan and Saudi Arabia back in the 1990s, according to Hill. Saudi Arabia, despite its status as a Western ally, for decades has been exporting to West and East Africa its Wahabi brand of purist Islam that, beyond the Middle Eastern kingdom's borders, has been taken to extremes.

Niger and Chad both have said they fear infiltration by Boko Haram. Boko Haram members from Nigeria and neighboring Niger were arrested in December in Cameroon, according to a report from Jacob Zenn, an analyst for The Jamestown Foundation and author of the report "Northern Nigeria's Boko Haram: The Prize in al-Qaeda's Africa Strategy." He quoted the imam of a grand mosque in southern Senegal as claiming that Boko Haram was recruiting local youths there in August 2012.

In a report written in January, before the military crackdown, Zenn said international collaboration between Boko Haram and militants in northern Mali, the Sahel, Somalia and other countries in the Muslim world have allowed Boko Haram to grow into an organization that "has now matched and even exceeded the capabilities of some al-Qaida affiliates."

$7 M Bounty on Boko Haram Leader's Head
November 4, 2013
By Haruna Umar and Michelle Faul

A Nigerian Islamic militant leader with an American $7-million bounty on his head boasts in a new video obtained Monday (November 4) that he commanded the Oct. 23 battle that killed at least 127 people a show of strength in the face of a nearly six-month-long military crackdown.

All but two victims were combatants killed during five hours of fierce fighting in the Yobe state capital, Damaturu. It was the first major attack in months on an urban center during an Islamic uprising that has terrorized northeast Nigeria.

Security forces swiftly freed major towns under the sway of the religious extremists after a state of emergency imposed in mid-May. But they have been struggling to hunt down Boko Haram militants in hideouts in local forests and caves and across borders with Cameroon, Chad and Niger, from which they emerge to attack schools and villages. Hundreds of civilians, mainly Muslims, have been killed by the militants in recent weeks, with some 40 killed in recent days.

People inspect burnt weapons following an attack by Boko Haram in Damaturu. Nigerian military and hospital reports indicate a 5-hour-long battle between Islamic extremists and troops in the capital of Nigeria's Yobe state killed at least 90 militants, 23 soldiers and eight police officers, October 28, 2013. (AP Photo)

Abubakar Shekau's video, dubbed The Battle of Damaturu, shows the bearded extremist leader in military camouflage, cradling an AK-47 automatic rifle and speaking in Arabic, Hausa and his native Kanuri as he sings the praises of Allah. The United States put a reward of $7 million dollars on Shekau's head in June, indicating the importance they give to the uprising that poses the biggest threat in decades to Nigeria's security.

"My brethren, this is the story I want to tell my brothers and the whole world: All this weaponry that you are seeing it is Allah who gave this to his worshippers who are fighting for Jihad all this ammunition was obtained in just one place," Shekau says.

The blurry video pans to a masked fighter standing amid hundreds of guns and ammunition belts and scores of boxes all of which Shekau claims was captured in Damaturu. He said he does not need to tell the world how many soldiers were killed and accuses the military of lying about its casualties. Nigeria's military says it killed a total of 95 insurgents and lost 22 soldiers and eight police officers that day, when the insurgents set ablaze four police command posts and an army barracks. An AP reporter who visited the mortuary counted 17 bodies in police uniform and 31 bodies said to belong to extremists.

Meanwhile, at least another 40 civilians were killed and hundreds of homes set ablaze in attacks by suspected militants over the last several days, the chairman of Bama local council in Borno state, Baba Shehu Gulumba, told reporters Monday in Maiduguri, the Borno state capital that once was a stronghold of the group.

Suspected Boko Haram sect member Muhammed Nazeef Yunus, an assistant lecturer, reacts as he is paraded by Nigeria secret police, in Abuja. Nigeria's intelligence agency paraded five suspected Islamic extremists including a university lecturer accused of plotting terrorism. Yunus, 44, denied that and told reporters that instead his lectures are against the network accused of killing hundreds of mainly Muslim civilian victims in northeast Nigeria in recent weeks. The northeast has been under a state of emergency since May, November 20, 2013. (AP Photo/Olamikan Gbemiga)

He said the attacks had huge economic costs with the worst fatalities in Bama town, where 27 civilians were killed on Thursday.

"Boko Haram burnt 300 houses, 20 shops, 204 livestock, 35 motorcycles, 15 cars , 250 sewing machines, 450 bags of cereal and cash estimated at 3.5 million naira (nearly $22,000)," in Bama, Gulumba said.

Another 13 people were killed at a highway junction in the area on Friday, he said. He appealed for more security forces to be deployed.

Bama, 70 kilometers (45 miles) from Maiduguri, is in the same area that suspected militants on Saturday attacked a wedding convoy, with authorities giving conflicting accounts of the death toll ranging from five to as many as 30, including the groom.

News of attacks is often slow to emerge since the military in May blocked cell phone services, saying the extremists were using the networks to coordinate attacks. Landlines don't work in Nigeria.

The battle in Damaturu overshadowed a major victory in which the military in neighboring Borno state said they bombed two "terrorist camps" and followed through with ground assaults that killed 74 insurgents while two soldiers were wounded.

Kidnapped French Priest Freed
December 31, 2013
By Elaine Ganley

A French priest kidnapped by Islamic radicals in northern Cameroon last November after ignoring danger warnings has been set free, President Francois Hollande's office said Tuesday (December 31).

Georges Vandenbeusch was kidnapped by heavily armed men on Nov. 13 in the far north of Cameroon, about 18 miles (30 kilometers) from the border with Nigeria. There was never a claim of responsibility, but suspicion fell on the radical Islamic sect Boko Haram which operates in the area, the Koza region, or on Ansaru, a Boko Haram splinter group responsible for most kidnappings of foreigners there.

The zone has been flagged as a risk for terrorism and kidnapping, but the priest - who cared for Nigerian refugees - chose to stay on to "exercise his mission," the French Foreign Ministry said at the time.

In a statement from his office, the French president thanked authorities in Cameroon and Nigeria for their "relentless" efforts in helping to free the priest. He "particularly" thanked Cameroon President Paul Biya for personally working on the case, but provided no details on how the release was secured.

Foreign Minister Laurent Fabius said on BFM-TV that he spoke to Biya regularly during the priest's captivity and the release came early Tuesday - with no ransom paid. Fabius traveled to Cameroon's capital, Yaounde, to bring Vandenbeusch home. The freed priest was expected back in France on Wednesday, New Year's Day.

Eyewitnesses said that a group of at least a dozen armed and masked gunmen had burst into the compound where Vandenbeusch lived and whisked him off on a motorbike, firing guns as they sped away. Two days after the priest was snatched, the kidnappers sent a representative to the area to demand the release of captured Boko Haram members, fellow priest Gilbert Pali said at the time.

Boko Haram has waged a campaign of bombings and shootings across Nigeria's north. The group has been held responsible for more than 790 deaths last year and many dozens more this year.

Father Georges Vandenbeusch addresses reporters after being greeted by French President Francois Hollande, left, upon his arrival at the Villacoublay military airport near Paris. The French priest was kidnapped by Islamic radicals in Cameroon and held for seven weeks, January 1, 2014. (AP Photo/Remy de la Mauviniere)

In April, a French expatriate family with four young children was kidnapped at gunpoint in the same far north region of Cameroon and freed two months later. Then, too, the captors demanded freedom for Boko Haram prisoners in custody in Nigeria and Cameroon, especially women and children.

There has been no announcement about freedom for prisoners to match the demands.

Each time French hostages are freed there is speculation about whether - or how much - ransom was paid. In the case of the family, Hollande reiterated French policy "that France does not pay ransom."

Fabius, the foreign minister, reiterated that policy on Tuesday. "It's longterm, very difficult team work" to free a hostage, he said. "There were discussions, of course," he said. "That is where Cameroon is extremely useful," he added, refusing to elaborate.

However, France has come under criticism over what diplomats and analysts say is an unofficial policy of indirectly paying ransom through middlemen. Vicki Huddleston, a former U.S. ambassador to Mali, has alleged that France paid a $17 million ransom to free hostages seized from a French mining site in Niger - cash she said ultimately funded al-Qaidalinked militants in neighboring Mali. The four hostages were freed in October.

Monsignor Bernard Podvin, spokesman for the bishops of France, said that Father Georges, as Vandenbeusch is called, "isn't someone who was seeking danger for danger's sake. He sought goodness."

Vatican spokesman the Rev. Federico Lombardi called for prayers for "all the other persons unjustly held hostage throughout the world."

The French statement announcing freedom for the priest noted that six French citizens continue to be held hostage in Mali and Syria.

Vandenbeusch was kidnapped less than two weeks after two French journalists were kidnapped then quickly shot to death in northern Mali.

Bring Back Our Girls

People attend a rally calling on the Government to rescue the school girls kidnapped from the Chibok Government secondary school, in Abuja, Nigeria. The president of Nigeria for weeks refused international help to search for more than 300 girls abducted from a school by Islamic extremists, one in a series of missteps that have led to growing international outrage against the government. The waiting has left parents in agony, especially since they fear some of their daughters have been forced into marriage with their abductors for a nominal bride price of $12. Boko Haram leader Abubakar Shekau called the girls slaves in a video and vowed to sell them", May 10, 2014. (AP Photo/Sunday Alamba)

At Least 100 Kidnapped from Girl's School
April 15, 2014
By Michelle Faul

Suspected Muslim extremists kidnapped about 100 girls Tuesday (April 15) from a school in northeastern Nigeria, less than a day after militants bombed a bus station and killed 75 people in the capital - a surge of violence that raised new doubts about the military's ability to contain an Islamic uprising.

With an 11-month-old state of emergency in three northeastern states failing to bring relief, the attacks are increasing calls for President Goodluck Jonathan to rethink his strategy in confronting the biggest threat to the security of Africa's most populous nation.

The attacks by the Boko Haram terrorist network have killed more than 1,500 people in this year alone, compared with an estimated 3,600 dead between 2010 and 2014.

In the latest attack, gunmen killed a soldier and a police officer guarding a school in Chibok on the edge of the Sambisa Forest and abducted the teenage girls after midnight, according to authorities.

Some of the girls escaped by jumping off the open truck as it was moving slowly along a road, according to an official who spoke on condition of anonymity because he was not authorized to talk to reporters.

Islamic extremists have been abducting girls to use as cooks and sex slaves.

All schools in Borno state were closed three weeks ago because of stepped-up attacks that have killed hundreds of students in the past year. But the young women - aged between 16 and 18 - were recalled to take their final exams, a local government official said.

Scores of protesters chanting "Bring Back Our Girls" marched in the Nigerian capital as many schools across the country closed to protest the abductions of schoolgirls by Boko Haram, the government's failure to rescue them and the killings of scores of teachers by Islamic extremists in recent years, May 22, 2014. (AP Photo/Sunday Alamba)

Boko Haram has targeted schools, mosques, churches, villages and agricultural centers in assaults that are increasingly indiscriminate. The insurgents have also made daring raids on military barracks and bases.

The report of the abductions came as officials were still dealing with the aftermath of Monday's bombing at the Abuja bus station that killed 75 and wounded 141, just miles from Nigeria's seat of government. The attack also was blamed on Boko Haram.

Hundreds of distraught people searching for missing loved ones gathered outside the morgue of Abuja's Asokoro Hospital, where they were shown photos of bombing victims.

"Innocent people are dying, for what they don't know," said Tina Eguaoje, who identified her relative, a police corporal, from among the pictures. She said he had just returned from a tour of duty in Liberia and was in his first day at the police academy.

M.D. Abubakar, the inspector general of police, urged Nigerians to come forward with any information to help track down those responsible for "this heinous crime." He said authorities were taking "stronger measures to review current security strategies and strengthen the safety of all parts of the country."

Last week, extremists staged their first reported attack in Jigawa state, to the west of the northeastern states where Boko Haram holds influence. They hit a police station, a Shariah Islamic court and a bank, and killed seven police officers.

Farther south, Gov. Gabriel Suswam of Benue state said traditional rivalries over land and water resources between mainly Christian farmers and predominantly Muslim herders are being exploited by militants. More than 200 people have been killed there in recent weeks.

"The belief I have, and which is shared by a lot of people, is that it is the same insurgents that are operating in other parts of the country that have found themselves in Benue, using the Fulani as a facade to unleash mayhem," Suswam told the Daily Trust newspaper.

Former Vice President Atiku Abubakar suggested it was time for the Nigerian government "to accept foreign assistance with fighting terrorism."

"The bombings ... automatically cast doubts on the (government) claims of containing the crisis to the fringes of the country," he said, urging stepped-up intelligence to pre-empt attacks.

Abubakar, who made his remarks in a statement responding to Monday's bombing, could not be reached to clarify his call. But it could be informed by a growing distrust of Nigeria's military by many northerners.

The country's two main political parties even have accused each other of supporting the Islamic insurgency for ulterior motives.

Jonathan said last year that he believes there are Boko Haram sympathizers and supporters even in his Cabinet and high ranks of the military. That was before he dismissed his entire military command in January, followed by the defense minister.

The New York-based World Policy Institute has identified northern politicians from both main parties who it says supported Boko Haram or were victims of extortion by the extremists.

People attend a demonstration calling on the government to rescue the kidnapped girls. Scores of protesters chanting "Bring Back Our Girls" marched in the Nigerian capital, May 22, 2014. (AP Photo/Sunday Alamba)

Some politicians have accused members of the military of colluding with Boko Haram, feeding the network information and arms, so that they can continue to steal from war coffers.

And some northern politicians say that keeping the insurgency going is a way to weaken the north as Nigeria gears up for elections in February 2015 that are shaping up as the biggest challenge to confront the governing People's Democratic Power since it won power in 1999 to end decades of military dictatorship.

Jonathan, a Christian from a minority tribe in the south, is expected to contend despite opposition even from within his own party, breaking an unwritten rule to alternate the presidency between a Christian southerner and a Muslim northerner.

In a country where relations between Muslims and Christians can be fraught and sometimes escalate into bloodshed, the 5-year-old insurgency is encouraging extremists from both religions and widening the gulf as never before.

The spiritual leader of Nigeria's more than 85 million Muslims said Sunday that there is no plot to Islamize the country, where another 85 million are Christians.

"Nobody can Islamize Nigeria. If Allah wanted, he would have made everybody Muslims, so also with Christianity," said Sa'ad Abubakar, the sultan of Sokoto. Abubakar is a common surname in Nigeria.

He said he hoped the government would take note of a stern statement last week from Jama'atu Nasril Islam, the country's biggest Muslim organization, which is headed by the sultan. It accused the military, which is notorious for human rights abuses, of killing Muslims "indiscriminately in the guise of fighting terrorism."

Jama'atu Nasril Islam alleged there is "a hidden grand agenda to destabilize Muslims in Nigeria."

For his part, Jonathan has said the Islamic uprising is a plot to destabilize his administration.

Transforming Nigeria into an Islamic state is Boko Haram's stated mission. It says that establishing Shariah law will halt the endemic corruption that keeps 70 percent of Nigerians impoverished while an elite lives in obscene luxury off oil proceeds.

Nigerians Search Forest for Girls
April 17, 2014
By Haruna Umar and Michelle Faul

Able-bodied men from the Nigerian town of Chibok have taken to the dangerous Sambisa Forest to search for more than 100 abducted girls and young women whom the military claimed to have freed from their Islamic extremist kidnappers, an education official said Thursday (April 17).

Six more have managed to escape their captors on their own, bringing to 20 the number that are free, the education commissioner of Borno state, Musa Inuwo Kubo, told reporters.

He spoke at a news conference where parents of the kidnapped students expressed their anguish over a Defense Ministry statement claiming to have freed all but eight of the students by Wednesday night.

"The military had really gladdened our hearts. But now we are left in confusion," said Lydia Ibrahim, whose three cousins are among the kidnapped. "These girls are innocent, we plead that government should do all that they can to help us."

Nigeria's chief of defense staff Air Marshal Alex S. Badeh, front, and other army chiefs wait to address the Nigerians Against Terrorism group during a demonstration calling on the government to rescue the kidnapped girls of the government secondary school in Chibok, May 26, 2014. (AP Photo/Gbenga Olamikan)

The Defense Ministry spokesman, Maj. Gen. Chris Olukolade, had said in a statement late Wednesday that the principal of the school from which the young women were abducted had confirmed that all but eight were freed.

But the principal, Asabe Kwambura, denied that to The Associated Press and flatly contradicted Olukolade, saying "Up till now we are still waiting and praying for the safe return of the students ... the security people, especially the vigilantes and the well-meaning volunteers of Gwoza are still out searching for them. The military people, too, are in the bush searching."

She said only 14 of those kidnapped by gunmen before dawn Tuesday have returned to Chibok - four who jumped from the back of a truck soon after the abductions and 10 who escaped into the bush when their abductors asked them to cook a meal.

Some of the escaped Kidnapped girls of the government secondary school Chibok, attend a meeting with Borno state governor, Kashim Shettima, in Maiduguri, June 2, 2014. (AP Photo/Jossy Ola)

Inuwo said six more girls have returned home - two found wandering in the forest by soldiers and four who had made their way to a village near where they were being held.

Olukolade, the defense spokesman, Thursday night retracted his statement, which he said had been based on a field report indicating "a major breakthrough." He added, "There is indeed no reason to play politics with the precious lives of the students. The number of those still missing is not the issue now as the life of every Nigerian is very precious."

A town official said people angry at the military's false statement and failure to find the abductees are taking the initiative and searching the forest themselves - dangerous because it is a known hiding place for militants of the Boko Haram extremist network and because it has been pounded by near-daily aerial bombardments by the air force.

Borno state Gov. Kashim Shettima offered a reward of $300,000 for information leading to the release of the students, aged between 16 and 18.

Shettima told the AP that he wanted to visit Chibok but the security forces told him it was too dangerous, even under military escort, for him to make the 130-kilometer (80-mile) drive from Maiduguri, the capital of Borno state and birthplace of Boko Haram.

Kwambura said the students were kidnapped because of a terrible mistake. She said the insurgents arrived after midnight at her Government Girls' Secondary School wearing military fatigues and posing as soldiers - a common tactic used by the insurgents. She said she believed them when they told her that they needed to move the girls for their own safety. So she allowed the extremists posing as soldiers to load the students on to the back of a truck.

It was only as the armed men were leaving, and started shooting, that she realized her mistake. The militants killed a soldier and a police officer guarding the school, she said.

The government closed all schools in Borno three weeks ago because of frequent attacks in which hundreds of students have been killed in the past year. The girls who were kidnapped had been recalled so they could write their final exams.

The extremists have been using abducted students as cooks, sex slaves and porters.

Boko Haram has been on a rampage this week, blamed for four attacks in three days that started with an explosion at a busy bus station during the Monday morning rush hour in Abuja, the capital, which killed at least 75 people.

Two attacks in northeastern villages killed 20 people Tuesday night and Wednesday morning.

More than 1,500 people have been killed this year, compared to an estimated 3,600 between 2010 and 2013.

The attacks undermine government and military claims that security forces are containing the Islamic militants' uprising that began five years ago in the extreme northeast of the country.

Boko Haram - the nickname means "Western education is sinful" - has vowed to force an Islamic state on Nigeria, Africa's most populous nation of some 170 million people divided almost equally between mainly Muslims in the north and a predominantly Christian south. They say Shariah law will halt corruption that is endemic.

230 Abducted Girls Still Missing
April 22, 2014
By Haruna Umar and Michelle Faul

A week after Islamic extremists stormed a remote boarding school in northeast Nigeria, more than 200 girls and young women remain missing despite a "hot pursuit" by security forces and an independent search by desperate fathers who headed into a dangerous forest to find their daughters.

Some of the escaped Kidnapped girls of the government secondary school Chibok, arrived for a meeting with Borno state governor, Kashim Shettima, in Maiduguri. Nigerian police say they have banned protests in the capital demanding that the government rescues the more than 200 girls still held captive by Boko Haram militants. Altine Daniel, a spokeswoman for Abuja police confirmed the ban in a text message, saying it was "because of security reasons," June 2, 2014. (AP Photo/Jossy Ola)

At Chibok, the scene of the attack, weeping parents cried on Monday (April 21), begging the kidnappers to "have mercy on our daughters," and for the government to rescue them. "I have not seen my dear daughter, she is a good girl," cried Musa Muka, whose 17-year-old Martha was taken away. "We plead with the government to help rescue her and her friends; we pray nothing happens to her."

Although at least 200 remain missing, dozens of the students managed to escape their captors, jumping from the back of an open truck after they were kidnapped in the pre-dawn hours of Tuesday last week or by running away and hiding in the dense forest. The number who escaped depends on whom you speak to - 39, 43, maybe more than 50.

The mass abduction is a major embarrassment for Nigeria's military, which had announced last week that security forces had rescued all but eight of those kidnapped - and then was forced to retract the statement. It came from Defense Ministry spokesman Maj. Gen. Chris Olukolade. "The operation is going on and we will continue to deploy more troops," Olukolade on Tuesday told The Associated Press, adding that air and land patrols are hunting for the students.

The Nigerian Air Force has halted what were near-daily air bombardments of the forest - presumably because of the kidnapped students. The extremists have abducted handfuls of students in recent months but this mass kidnapping is unprecedented.

Nigeria's military is already confronted by mounting criticism over its failure to curb the 5-year-old Islamic uprising despite having draconian powers under an 11-month state of emergency in three northeastern states covering one-sixth of the country. It seems every time the military trumpets a success in its "onslaught on terrorists," the extremists step up the tempo and deadliness of attacks. More than 1,500 people have been killed in the insurgency so far this year, compared to an estimated 3,600 between 2010 and 2013.

Military and government claims that the extremists were cornered in the remote northeast were shattered by a massive explosion April 14 at a bus station in Abuja, the capital in the center of the country, which killed at least 75 people and wounded 141.

The leader of the homegrown Boko Haram terrorist network, Abubakar Shekau, in a video received Saturday claimed responsibility for the Abuja bombing but said nothing about the kidnapped girls. Shekau repeated his opposition to "corrupting" Western influences, saying. "Everyone that calls himself a Muslim must stop obeying the constitution, must abandon democracy, must stay away from Western education." Boko Haram means "Western education is sinful" in the local Hausa language.

The Islamic insurgency has forced some 750,000 people including hundreds of thousands of farmers to flee their homes, raising fears of a food shortage. Refugees in neighboring countries said they were escaping militant attacks as well as the often brutal response of Nigeria's military.

In Chibok town, even the number of students abducted is in question. Education officials had said 129 - which was the number of students writing an exam. The girls had been recalled to write a physics exam as the school, and all schools in Borno state, were closed four weeks ago by the government because of the increased attacks. But as parents rushed from across Borno state to the boarding school, the number of missing grew. On Monday, parents gave the visiting Borno governor a list of 234 missing girls and young women, aged between 16 and 18.

Women attend a demonstration in Lagos calling on the government to rescue kidnapped school girls. The first of Nigeria's kidnapped "Chibok girls" to make it home Sept. 25, 2014, after being released by her Islamic extremist captors spent a tortured night, tossing and turning and screaming "They will kill me! They will kill me!" So says the Rev. Enoch Mark, who stayed up through the night with the traumatized young woman, May 5, 2014. (AP Photo/ Sunday Alamba, File)

School principal Asabe Kwambura told The Associated Press the number of students accounted for is 43 and the number missing is 230. The extremists set the school ablaze, leaving only burned-out shells.

As confidence in the military eroded, the parents and other Chibok residents pooled money to buy fuel for motorcycles and headed into the Sambisa Forest, a nearby known hideout of extremists.

A parent who did not give his name described the civilian search to Borno state Gov. Kashim Shettima when he visited Chibok on Monday. The father said they pursued the abductors some 50 kilometers (30 miles) deep into the forest, getting directions from villagers and a lone herdsman, who all said they had seen the girls. The father described thick forest with trees blocking the sun and sky. Then they came to a fork in the footpath and saw an elderly man.

"He confirmed to us that he saw our daughters, with their kidnappers. He said the girls were brought down from the truck and made to trek into the forest. He pointed to us the direction they took them, but warned us that if we ventured into that part of the forest without any security personnel we would all be killed together with our daughters."

At that point the search party returned to Chibok, he said. Some got lost in the forest and took three days to get back to the town on foot.

School girls who escaped abduction from the Chibok government secondary school attend a meeting with Nigeria President Goodluck Jonathan, in Abuja. The Nigerian president met for the first time with parents of 219 kidnapped Nigerian schoolgirls and dozens of classmates who managed to escape from their Islamic extremist captors. Jonathan assured them of his determination that those still in captivity "are brought out alive," presidential spokesman Reuben Abati told reporters after the meeting, July 22, 2014. (AP Photo)

He said they never once encountered any soldiers. And the only security in Chibok is a handful of police officers, according to education officials.

Abducted Girls Married to Militants
April 30, 2014
By Michelle Faul

Scores of girls and young women kidnapped from a school in Nigeria are being forced to marry their Islamic extremist abductors, a civic organization reported Wednesday (April 30).

At the same time, the Boko Haram terrorist network is negotiating over the students' fate and is demanding an unspecified ransom for their release, a Borno state community leader told The Associated Press.

He said the Wednesday night message from the abductors also claimed that two of the girls have died from snake bites.

The message was sent to a member of a presidential committee mandated last year to mediate a ceasefire with the Islamic extremists, said the civic leader, who spoke on condition of anonymity because he is not authorized to speak about the talks.

Journalists photograph as people hold a vigil to mark one month after the girls of government secondary school Chibok were kidnapped, in Abuja. Nigeria's government is ruling out an exchange of more than 270 kidnapped schoolgirls for detained Islamic militants, Britain's top official for Africa said. Boko Haram abducted more than 300 schoolgirls from the school in Chibok in the northeastern state of Borno on April 15. May 14, 2014. (AP Photo/Sunday Alamba)

The news of negotiations comes as parents say the girls are being sold into marriage to Boko Haram militants. The students are being paid 2,000 naira ($12) to marry the fighters, Halite Aliyu of the Borno-Yobe People's Forum told The Associated Press. She said the parents' information about mass weddings is coming from villagers in the Sambisa Forest, on Nigeria's border with Cameroon, where Boko Haram is known to have hideouts.

"The latest reports are that they have been taken across the borders, some to Cameroon and Chad," Aliyu said. It was not possible to verify the reports about more than 200 missing girls kidnapped in the northeast by the Boko Haram terrorist network two weeks ago.

"Some of them have been married off to insurgents. A medieval kind of slavery. You go and capture women and then sell them off," community elder

Pogu Bitrus of Chibok, the town where the girls were abducted, told the BBC Hausa Service.

Outrage over the failure to rescue the girls is growing and hundreds of women braved heavy rain to march Wednesday to Nigeria's National Assembly to protest lack of action over the students. Hundreds more also marched in Kano, Nigeria's second city in the north.

"The leaders of both houses said they will do all in their power but we are saying two weeks already have past, we want action now," said activist Mercy Asu Abang.

"We want our girls to come home alive - not in body bags," she said.
Nigerians have harnessed social media to protest, trending under the hashtag #BringBackOurGirls.

There also has been no news of 25 girls kidnapped from Konduga town in Borno state earlier this month.

A federal senator from the region said the military is aware of the movements of the kidnappers and the girls because he has been feeding them details that he has gathered on a near-daily basis.

"What bothered me the most is that whenever I informed the military where these girls were, after two to three days they were moved from that place to another. Still, I would go back and inform them on new developments," Sen. Ahmad Zanna is quoted as saying at the Nigerian online news site Persecond News.

Zanna said some of the girls are in Kolofata in Cameroon, about 15 kilometers (nine miles) from the border with Nigeria. He said one of the insurgents had called a friend in Borno state to say that he had just got married and was settling in Kolofata. Zanna also said three or four days ago Nigerian herdsmen reported seeing the girls taken in boats onto an island in Lake Chad.

Another senator from the region said the government needs to get international help to rescue the girls. The government must do "whatever it takes, even seeking external support to make sure these girls are released," Sen. Ali Ndume said. "The longer it takes the dimmer the chances of finding them, the longer it takes the more traumatized the family and the abducted girls are."

About 50 of the kidnapped girls managed to escape from their captors in the first days after their abduction, but some 220 remain missing, according to the principal of the Chibok Girls Secondary School, Asabe Kwambura. They are between 16 and 18 years old and had been recalled to the school to write a physics exam.

The failure to rescue the girls is a massive embarrassment to Nigeria's government and the military, already confronted by mounting criticism over its apparent inability to curb the 5-year-old Islamic uprising despite having draconian powers through an 11-month state of emergency in three northeastern states covering one-sixth of the country.

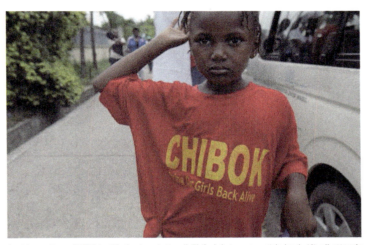

A girl wearing a T-Shirt with the inscription " Chibok brings our girls back Alive" attends a demonstration in Lagos calling on government to rescue the kidnapped school girls. Scores of girls are being forced to marry their Islamic extremist abductors, a civic organization reported. At the same time, the Boko Haram terrorist network is negotiating over the students' fate and is demanding an unspecified ransom for their release, a Borno state community leader told The Associated Press. He said the Wednesday night message from the abductors also claimed that two of the girls have died from snake bites. The message was sent to a member of a presidential committee mandated last year to mediate a ceasefire with the Islamic extremists, said the civic leader, who spoke on condition of anonymity because he is not authorized to speak about the talks, May 1, 2014. (AP Photo/ Sunday Alamba)

The military trumpets a success in its "onslaught on terrorists" but then the extremists step up the tempo and deadliness of their attacks. More than 1,500 people have been killed in the insurgency so far this year, compared to an estimated 3,600 between 2010 and 2013.

President Goodluck Jonathan, who is from the predominantly Christian south of Nigeria, has been accused of insensitivity to the plight of people in the north, who are mainly Muslims.

People from Nigeria's northeast feel that they are being punished because they did not vote for Jonathan's People's Democratic Party - the entire region is held by opposition politicians, said Aliyu, of the Borno-Yobe People's Forum. "The northeast zone is in flames and nothing is being done because we didn't vote PDP," she said. "Women are raped daily, our children are being carted away like animals and sold like chickens, they (extremists) burn schools, they burn mosques, they raze entire villages."

Nana Shettima, the wife of Borno Governor, Kashim Shettima, center, weeps as she speaks with school girls from the government secondary school Chibok that were kidnapped by the Islamic extremist group Boko Haram, and later escaped in Chibok Nigeria. The plight of the remaining 276 kidnapped girls — and the failure of the Nigerian military to find them — has drawn international attention to an escalating Islamic extremist insurrection that has killed more than 1,500 so far this year, May 5, 2014. (AP Photo)

She said it would take decades to rebuild from the destruction that has forced an estimated 750,000 people from their homes, some into neighboring countries, fleeing the terror of the zealots as well as abuses by the soldiers.

The military's lack of progress in rescuing the girls indicates that large parts of northeastern Nigeria remain beyond the control of the government. Until the kidnappings, the air force had been mounting near-daily bombing raids since mid-January on the Sambisa Forest and mountain caves bordering Chad.

Aliyu said that in northeastern Nigeria "life has become nasty, short and brutish. We are living in a state of anarchy."

This file image taken from video by Boko Haram, shows the alleged missing girls abducted from Chibok, May 12, 2014. (AP Photo/File)

People attend a demonstration calling on the government to rescue the kidnapped schoolgirls of the Chibok secondary school. A Nigerian government official said "all options are open" in efforts to rescue almost 300 abducted schoolgirls from their captors as US reconnaissance aircraft started flying over this West African country in a search effort. Boko Haram, the militant group that kidnapped the girls last month from a school in Borno state, had released a video yesterday purporting to show some of the girls. A civic leader said representatives of the missing girls' families were set to view the video as a group later today to see if some of the girls can be identified, May 13, 2014. (AP Photo / Sunday Alamba)

Michelle Obama Calls for Return of Girls
May 7, 2014
By Darlene Superville

Michelle Obama is adding her voice to worldwide calls for the safe return of nearly 300 kidnapped Nigerian schoolgirls.

The first lady says on Twitter that, quote, "our prayers are with the missing Nigerian girls and their families." She also says "it's time to bring back our girls."

Joy Bishara, one of two school girls who escaped being kidnapped by Islamist extremists by jumping off a truck, is photographed outside her home, in Chibok, May 18, 2014. (AP Photo/Sunday Alamba)

Mrs. Obama packaged her tweet with a photo of herself in the White House holding a white piece of paper with the message "(hashtag) Bring Back Our Girls" written in black, capital letters.

The tweet was signed "-mo," indicating that she sent it herself.

The U.S. is sending technical experts to Nigeria to help authorities find the girls.

The girls were abducted from their school more than three weeks ago by an Islamist extremist group whose leader has threatened to sell them.

First lady Michelle Obama meets with issue experts about international girls' education in Washington. The first lady spoke about the importance of education girls and about the kidnapped girls in Nigeria, May 22, 2014. (AP Photo/Jacquelyn Martin)

Selma Hayek at Cannes
May 23, 2014
By Nekesa Mumbi Moody

When Salma Hayek walked the Cannes Film Festival red carpet holding up the sign "Bring Back Our Girls," the cast of "The Expendables" followed suit the next night - even if some of them didn't know what the slogan was about.

"I remember Victor (Ortiz) was like, 'What were those signs?' and I had to fill him in,'" actor Kellan Lutz of his co-star.

Ortiz, Hayek and others helped spread the message, a plea for the return of nearly 300 girls kidnapped in Nigeria by the Islamist extremist group Boko Haram, by using one of the most famous media events in the world. The "Bring Back Our Girls" campaign has become a hashtag on Twitter and championed by luminaries including U.S. first lady Michelle Obama.

Still, it wasn't the only social message at Cannes this year. The actors and director of the Turkish film "Winter Sleep" held up signs reading "Soma," referring to the recent Turkish mining tragedy that killed 301 miners.

In an interview with The Associated Press this week, Angelina Jolie, known for her activism, worried that stars promoting the "Bring Back Our Girls" campaign could backfire.

"We need to not turn the Boko Haram into superstars that get more attention for doing something so horrible," she said. "We need to go after them, arrest and they need to face justice.

"Because at the end of the day, the bigger picture is this kind of horror happens around the world. Women are facing this kind of abuse, so are men and boys. And the answer cannot be simply one situation and that will solve it."

Actress Salma Hayek, center, holds up a sign reading "bring back our girls" as she arrives for the screening of Saint-Laurent at the 67th international film festival, Cannes, southern France. At left is director Paul Brizzi, second left, director Roger Allers, second right director Joan C. Gratz and director Gaetan Brizzi, May 17, 2014. (AP Photo/Thibault Camus)

"I would beg the media, for all of us, to not treat things one at a time," she added.

Other stars were supportive of using the Cannes stage to promote something more serious than films.

"It's a great place. Wherever you can let people know that's wrong, you can't do that," said actor Chris Tucker.

Actor Viggo Mortensen, who held up a flag of his soccer team at his Cannes photo call for the movie "Jauja," had no problem with other celebrities doing the same for something weightier.

"I have no problem speaking out when it seems appropriate or called for - I've done it before," he said.

Hayek held up the sign as she walked the red carpet for her animated film "The Prophet." She said it was not out of character.

"I was always involved in women's rights before I was a celebrity," she said. "But of course (the premiere) was a good opportunity to use it to continue to put pressure on the governments so that they bring back our girls."

Lutz said the "Expendables" cast were handed the signs before they walked the carpet but he was already supportive of the campaign.

"To do it on one of the most watched locations and spots where people in the films are just walking up, and it's just such an iconic location ... it impacts so much," he said.

Martha Mark, the mother of kidnapped school girl Monica Mark cries, in the family house, in Chibok, May 19, 2014. (AP Photo/Sunday Alamba)

Malala Visits Nigeria
July 14, 2014
By Lekan Oyekanmi and Michelle Faul

The Pakistani teen who survived a Taliban assassination attempt in 2012 marked her 17th birthday Monday (July 14) with a visit to Nigeria and urged Islamic extremists to free the 219 schoolgirls who were kidnapped there, calling them her "sisters."

Malala Yousafzai, who has become an international symbol for women's rights in the face of hard-line Islam, said Nigeria's president promised to meet for the first time with the abducted girls' parents.

"My birthday wish this year is 'Bring Back Our Girls' now and alive," she said, using the social media slogan that has been picked up around the world to demand freedom for the girls, who were abducted by the extremist group Boko Haram in April from a school in the remote northeast Nigerian town of Chibok.

Pakistani activist Malala Yousafzai, left, poses for a photograph with Nigerian President, Goodluck Jonathan, right, at the Presidential villa, in Abuja. Yousafzai on Monday won a promise from Nigeria's leader to meet with the parents of some of the 219 schoolgirls held by Islamic extremists for three months. Malala celebrated her 17th birthday on Monday in Nigeria with promises to work for the release of the girls, July 14, 2014. (AP Photo)

Malala appealed directly to their captors as she held hands with some of the girls who escaped.

"Lay down your weapons. Release your sisters. Release my sisters. Release the daughters of this nation. Let them be free. They have committed no crime."

She added: "You are misusing the name of Islam ... Islam is a religion of peace."

Malala also spoke against the custom of child brides in her home country, a tradition common in Nigeria, too. Boko Haram has threatened to sell some of the girls as brides if its fighters are not freed.

"Protect girls from cruelty," she said in a speech, explaining that girls should not be forced to marry or to leave school to become brides "when they should be girls," or to give birth to children "when they themselves are children."

Boko Haram attacks continued over the weekend with witnesses blaming the group for the bombing of a major bridge on a northeast Nigerian highway that further limits access to its base camps in the Sambisa Forest, where it is believed to be holding some of the girls.

Gunmen destroyed most of the bridge on the road between Maiduguri and Biu on Saturday night, making it impossible for vehicles to cross, the spokesman for the Nigerian Vigilante Group, Abbas Gava, told The Associated Press.

Malala met Monday with Nigeria's President Goodluck Jonathan and told reporters that the president "promised me that the girls will be returned as soon as possible."

She described an emotional meeting Sunday with some of the girls' parents.

"I could see tears in their eyes. They were hopeless. But they seem to have this hope in their hearts," and they were asking if they could meet the president.

Jonathan has not met with any of the parents, though some regularly make the dangerous drive from Chibok to join activists who have held daily rallies in Abuja.

When the activists tried to march peacefully to the presidential villa in May, they were blocked by soldiers and police. Jonathan canceled a planned trip to Chibok that same month.

On Monday, he told Malala that criticism that his government is not doing enough is "wrong and misplaced," according to a presidential statement.

"The great challenge in rescuing the Chibok girls is the need to ensure that they are rescued alive," he said, insisting his government is "actively pursuing all feasible options" to achieve their safe return.

Boko Haram leader Abubakar Shekau put out a new video Sunday in which he repeated demands that the government release detained insurgents in exchange for the girls' freedom.

"Nigerians are saying 'Bring Back Our Girls,' and we are telling Jonathan to bring back our arrested warriors, our army," he said in the video, which was obtained by the AP through similar channels used for previous messages.

Jonathan so far has refused, despite pleas from the parents.

Since the mass abduction, Boko Haram has increased the number and deadliness of its attacks with a two-pronged approach - bombing cities and towns and a scorched-earth strategy in villages, gunning down villagers, looting livestock and burning down huts.

In the new video, Shekau crowed over recent victories, including two explosions at a fuel depot in Lagos that the government tried to cover up. It would be the first reported bombing by Boko Haram in Lagos - Nigeria's commercial capital, an Atlantic port and probably the continent's most populous city with some 20 million people. The attack also raises fears that the insurgency is spreading beyond its stronghold at the opposite end of the country.

School girls who escaped abduction from the Chibok government secondary school arrive for a meeting with Nigeria President Goodluck Jonathan, in Abuja, July 22, 2014. (AP Photo)

At least four people died in the June 25 blasts, including an alleged female suicide bomber, according to Western diplomats who spoke on condition of anonymity because of the sensitivity of the issue.

Shekau also claimed responsibility for another bomb that went off hours before at the biggest shopping mall in Nigeria's capital, Abuja, killing at least 21 people.

On Monday, Malala also appealed to the Nigerian government to dedicate more money to education and to drastically reduce the hundreds of thousands of children who are out of school throughout the country, not just in the area targeted by Boko Haram.

The group's nickname means "Western education is sinful." Boko Haram wants to enforce an Islamic state in Nigeria, whose 170 million people are almost equally divided between Christians in the south and Muslims in the north.

Missing Girl's Parents Refuse to Meet Goodluck Jonathan
July 15, 2014
By Lekan Oyekanmi and Michelle Faul

Parents and schoolmates of the 219 schoolgirls held captive by Boko Haram extremists refused at the last minute Tuesday (July 15) to meet with Nigeria's President Goodluck Jonathan, who accused activists of "playing politics."

"It now appears that our fight to get the girls of Chibok back is not only a fight against a terrorist insurgency, but also against a political opposition," Jonathan said in a statement.

The mass abduction April 15, exactly three months ago, has been plagued by politics from the start. First lady Patience Jonathan charged the kidnappings never occurred and were being fabricated by her husband's enemies to damage his image.

She also had two leading activists briefly arrested, and relations between the government, security forces and the #BringBackOurGirls movement have been tense ever since.

At one point in May when the activists tried to stage a peaceful march to present their demands to Jonathan, they were blocked by soldiers and police.

On Tuesday, security agents locked the doors to the National Assembly, preventing the campaigners from attending a scheduled meeting with the Senate president, said Rotimi Olawale, a spokeswoman for the campaign.

It seems the campaigners then persuaded the parents and girls not to meet with the president, who has faced international condemnation for his slow response to mount a campaign to rescue the girls.

"My priority is not politics. My priority is the return of these girls," Jonathan's statement said. He accused the Nigerian chapter of the Bring Back Our Girls campaign of "psychological terrorism ... playing politics with the situation and the grief of the parents and the girls. They should be ashamed of their actions."

Jonathan has never met with the parents or the escaped girls, though they have been asking to meet with him for weeks. In May, he canceled without explanation a trip to Chibok, the remote northeast town where the girls were kidnapped.

Politics probably played a part in that cancellation since Chibok is in the northeastern state of Borno, which is governed by an opposition politician very critical of Jonathan.

Nigeria President, Goodluck Jonathan, left, greets some school girls who escaped abduction from the Chibok government secondary school. The Nigerian president met for the first time with parents of 219 kidnapped Nigerian schoolgirls and dozens of classmates who managed to escape from their Islamic extremist captors. Jonathan assured them of his determination that those still in captivity "are brought out alive," presidential spokesman Reuben Abati told reporters after the meeting, July 22, 2014. (AP Photo)

On Monday, Nigeria's leader promised Pakistani activist Malala Yousafzai that he would meet the parents. Malala said that was the parents' wish, that they wanted the support of their president.

"I want to be clear, this government stands with complete solidarity with the girls and their parents. We are doing everything in our power to bring back our girls," he said Tuesday after the meeting was cancelled. "As a father of girls, I stand ready to meet with the parents of our abducted children and the truly brave girls that have escaped this nightmare through the grace of God."

Alicia Keys Holds Protest for Lost Girls
October 14, 2014
By Mesfin Fekadu

Alicia Keys held a protest in New York City on Tuesday (October 14) to raise awareness about the 200-plus Nigerian schoolgirls who were kidnapped by Boko Haram militants in April.

Tuesday marked six months since the girls were abducted. Keys kicked off a protest with 30 others at the consulate general of Nigeria, holding signs that read "We Are Here" and "Safe Schools Now!"

Singer-songwriter Alicia Keys takes a "selfie" as she joins protesters with the "Bring Back Our Girls" campaign marking the six month anniversary of the kidnapping in front of the Nigerian consulate in New York, October 14, 2014. (AP Photo/Kathy Willens)

They chanted "Bring back our girls" and "When do we want them? Now! Now! Alive!" as New Yorkers walked up the street during lunch hour, while others stopped to capture photos and video.

Keys, who is pregnant, said in an interview that she felt touched to take action because she is a mother. Her son, Egypt, turned 4 on Tuesday.

"Today is my son's birthday and it is also making me stand in solidarity with all the mothers of the Chibok girls who have been abducted for six months and are still missing. And it is just outrageous that that's going on," the 33-year-old said as others chanted behind her.

Keys recently launched the movement "We Are Here," which fights for social justice. She also recorded and released a song with the same name.

She was joined by her husband, producer-rapper Swizz Beatz. She said people need a reminder that the schoolgirls are still missing.

"Some people have even told me they've heard things about 'there's been progress,' but there hasn't been progress because the girls aren't back," Keys said. "So I think that we get mixed information. We don't know, so we just have to keep being made aware of what's happening."

A woman attends a demonstration in Abuja, Nigeria, calling on the government to rescue the kidnapped girls, September 11, 2014. (AP Photo/Olamikan Gbemiga)

Most of the Girls Still Missing
February 11, 2015
By Chika Oduah

When Islamic extremists snatched more than 270 girls from the Chibok boarding school in Nigeria in the dead of night, protests broke out worldwide. The U.S. pledged to help find them, and the #BringBackOurGirls hashtag was born.

Some 10 months later, most are still missing. The Boko Haram extremist group sees the mass kidnapping as a shining symbol of success, and has abducted hundreds of other girls, boys and women. The militants brag to their new captives with claims that the Chibok girls surrendered, converted to Islam and married fighters.

"They told me the Chibok girls have a new life where they learn to fight," says Abigail John, 15, who was held by Boko Haram for more than four weeks before escaping. "They said we should be like them and accept Islam."

The kidnappings reflect the growing ambition and brazenness of Boko Haram, which seeks to impose an Islamic state across Nigeria, Africa's most populous country. Some 10,000 people have died in the Islamic uprising over the past year, compared to 2,000 in the previous four years, according to the U.S. Council on Foreign Relations.

Maj. Gen. Chris Olukolade, Nigeria's top military spokesman speaks during an interview in Abuja. Days after Nigeria's military raised hopes by announcing Islamic extremists have agreed to a cease-fire, Boko Haram is still fighting and there is no word about 219 schoolgirls held hostage for six months. Officials had said talks with Nigeria's Islamic extremist rebels would resume in neighboring Chad this week, October 22, 2014. (AP Photo/Jon Gambrell, File)

"It's devastating," said Bukky Shonibare, an activist in Abuja, of the kidnappings. "It makes you wonder, what is being done?"

John was among three girls interviewed by The Associated Press who recently escaped from Boko Haram. While their stories could not be independently verified, they were strikingly similar, and all spoke of their captors' obsession with the Chibok girls.

The girls had no idea whether the militants were telling the truth or making up stories to taunt their victims. John says the fighters enjoyed relating how they had whipped and slapped the Chibok girls until they submitted.

When the Nigerian air force dropped a bomb on the house where John was confined, she tried to escape, she says. She wrestled with the fighters, but they broke her am and hauled her off to another house.

At the end of last year, the Nigerian army liberated the town where she was held. She is now in Yola with her father, sister and six brothers, in a house overcrowded with refugees. She finally was able to get medical attention for her fractured right arm, which remains in a cast.

The kidnappings of the Chibok girls in April brought Boko Haram to the world's attention in a way the group could not have imagined. The hashtag #BringBackOurGirls was tweeted more than 480,000 times globally in early May, and U.S. first lady Michelle Obama held it up in a sign to television cameras. She said at the time, "In these girls, Barack and I see our own daughters …we can only imagine the anguish their parents are feeling right now."

On Wednesday, Nigerian President Goodluck Jonathan again promised the girls will be brought home alive, saying he is "more hopeful" about their fate now that a multinational force is being formed to fight Boko Haram.

"Give us some time over the Chibok girls. The story will be better in a few weeks," Jonathan promised, as he has many times in the past, on a nationally televised program.

In the 10 months since the mass kidnapping, Boko Haram has increased the tempo and ferocity of its insurgency. In August, it began seizing and holding towns, and - copying the Islamic State group - declared it would recreate an ancient Islamic caliphate in the region. The fighting has since spilled across Nigeria's borders, and the African Union this month authorized a multinational force of 8,750 troops to try to stamp it out.

In his file image taken from video released by Boko Haram, Abubakar Shekau, center, the leader of Nigeria's Islamic extremist group denies agreeing to any cease-fire with the government and says more than 200 kidnapped schoolgirls all have converted to Islam and been married off, October 31, 2014. (AP Photo/Boko Haram, File)

Dorcas Aiden, 20, was another of those caught in Boko Haram's siege. She had finished high school and was living at home when the war came to her village. Fighters took her to a house in the town of Gulak and held her captive for two weeks last September.

The more than 50 teenage girls crammed into the house were beaten if they refused to study Quranic verses or conduct daily Muslim prayers, she says. When the fighters got angry, they shot their guns in the air. Aiden finally gave in and denied her Christian faith to become Muslim, at least in name, she says.

One day, the fighters stormed into the room where she was kept locked up with a dozen other girls. They showed a video of the Chibok girls, dressed in hijabs, with only their faces visible through their veils. Aiden says she was so overwhelmed that she cried.

The fighters said the Chibok girls were all Muslims now, and some were training as fighters to fight women, which Boko Haram men are not supposed to do.

Aiden's captors boasted about how they had married off the Chibok girls, she says. One fighter said he would marry her. She balked.

"I said, 'No, I will not marry you,'" Aiden recounts. "So he pulled out a gun and beat my hand."

Aiden says the insurgents threatened to break the legs of any girl who tried to escape, but she and six others ran anyway. As she made her way through abandoned farm fields, she noticed that Boko Haram had filled about 10 other

Aiden, who is now in Yola with tens of thousands of other refugees, dreams of going to university, in defiance of the extremists' insistence that girls should be married, not educated. The nickname Boko Haram means "Western education is forbidden or sinful."

Another escapee, a shy 16-year-old captured in September, begs that her name not be published because she escaped only a few weeks ago and believes the fighters are actively searching for her. After the girl's village was attacked four times, she fled to a great-aunt. Then that village also was targeted, she says.

The fighters held her for four months. When she escaped, she walked through the bush and across the border into Cameroon to avoid areas under Boko Haram's control. She is now taking refuge in a Catholic church in Yola.

All the girls say they were not raped, despite the fears of some villagers. Instead, the fighters said they wanted the girls to remain virgins until they were married off.

"They said they are doing the work of God, so they will not touch us," the 16-year-old recounts.

As she tells her story, she fidgets and looks down at her hands, clasped in her lap. She recounts how one fighter, nicknamed "Tall Arab," was set on marrying her. She pleaded that she was too young, but was told, "Do you think you are better than those Chibok girls that we kidnapped?"

The man told her the Chibok girls were "enjoying their matrimonial homes," she remembers. He also said the Chibok girls had turned against their parents, and were "ready to slit their parents' throats" if they ever saw them again.

Some never will. Even if the girls are released, people in Chibok say at least 13 of their parents have died since they were seized, in Boko Haram violence or possibly stress-related illness.

While dozens of Chibok girls escaped on their own after their kidnapping, 219 are still missing. Nigeria's military initially feared any action could lead to the girls being killed. But villagers reported last week that air force jets have begun bombing the Sambisa Forest - the area where fighters told Aiden some girls still are held captive.

Joining the Islamic State Group

Islamic State group militants hold up their flag as they patrol in a commandeered Iraqi military vehicle in Fallujah, Iraq, March 30, 2014. (AP Photo, File)

Adopting Islamic State Methods
March 2, 2015
By Michelle Faul and Haruna Umar

The latest video from Nigeria's Boko Haram Islamic extremist group shows the bodies of two beheaded men accused of spying, and copies some of the hallmarks of propaganda from the Islamic State group.

The SITE intelligence group said the video called "Harvest of Spies" was posted Monday on Twitter by Boko Haram's new media arm. The video is much slicker than previous ones and SITE said it borrows certain elements from IS productions, such as the sound of a beating heart and heavy breathing immediately before the execution.

Boko Haram has said in social media messages last month that it is considering swearing allegiance to IS.

Monday's video shows a man identified as Dawoud Muhammad of Baga city on his knees in the bush before several armed and masked fighters. In response to questions, Muhammad says a police officer paid him 5,000 naira ($25) to spy and promised to make him so rich he would never have to farm again. The other man is identified as Muhammad Awlu.

The video does not show the actual beheadings but the two bodies after the executions, with heads on the chests.

Boko Haram previously published only one beheading, of a Nigerian fighter pilot whose plane went missing in September.

Boko Haram's violent campaign in Nigeria killed at least 10,000 people last year, according to the Council on Foreign Affairs. At least 1.6 million people have been driven from their homes in the group's brutal 6-year uprising to create an Islamic state in Nigeria, Africa's most populous nation of 160 million people divided between mainly Muslims in the north and Christians in the south.

Boko Haram began emulating the Islamic State group last August, declaring it had established an Islamic caliphate in territory it controls in northeastern Nigeria.

In a major turnabout, Nigeria's military in recent weeks has wrested back a score of towns and villages that had been under the control of the insurgents for months.

Chad and Niger in the Fight
March 9, 2015
By Krista Larson

Soldiers from Chad and Niger launched the largest international push to defeat Nigeria's Islamic extremists whose war has spilled over into neighboring countries, officials and witnesses said Monday. Chad's president has warned that the leader of Boko Haram must surrender or be killed.

At least 200 vehicles full of soldiers were spotted by residents crossing from Niger into Nigeria. Loud detonations were soon heard, signaling heavy combat with Boko Haram, said Adam Boukarna, a resident of the border town of Bosso, Niger.

The push marks a sharp escalation by African nations against Boko Haram nearly six years after the group began its insurrection. At an African Union summit in Addis Ababa, Ethiopia on Jan. 31, African leaders agreed to send 7,500 troops to fight Boko Haram. Later neighboring countries agreed to increase the force to 8,750. U.N. Secretary General Ban Ki Moon has said he supports the AU's move.

Chadian troops participate in the closing ceremony of operation Flintlock in an army base in N'djamena, Chad. The U.S. military and its Western partners conduct this training annually and set up plans long before Boko Haram began attacking its neighbors Niger, Chad and Cameroon. Chadian Brig. Gen. Zakaria Ngobongue said Monday that his soldiers alongside troops from Niger had entered Nigeria but he declined to give further details about the ongoing operation. Ngobongue described Boko Haram fighters as "bandits and criminals who have nothing to do with religion", March 9, 2015. (AP Photo/Jerome Delay)

The new offensive includes troops from Niger for the first time, in addition to Chadian forces that were already carrying out missions in Nigeria, Chadian Brig. Gen. Zakaria Ngobongue said Monday. He described extremism as a "cancer" in the region that could not be defeated by any one country alone.

"They are bandits and criminals who have nothing to do with religion," Ngobongue said, speaking to reporters after the closing ceremony for Flintlock, an annual training exercise in counter-insurgency tactics involving some 20 countries.

U.S. Army Gen. David M. Rodriguez, commander of the U.S. Africa Command which sponsored the exercise, noted here on Monday that the Islamic insurgents have been operating not very far from this dusty capital: The group has carried out attacks on this year as close as about 150 kilometers

(90 miles) away. N'Djamena is about 30 kilometers (18 miles) from the Nigerian border.

"We find this year's exercise both unique and relevant because as you know we are not far from the immediate threat of Boko Haram," the American general, who had earlier commanded U.S. military forces in Afghanistan, told reporters.

Nigeria and its allies will defeat Boko Haram, said Mike Omeri, the Nigerian government spokesman on the insurgency.

Boko Haram's announcement over the weekend that it is affiliated to the Islamic State extremist group "is an act of desperation and comes at a time when Boko Haram is suffering heavy losses at the hands of the Nigerian Armed Forces and its regional partners," said Omeri. "The fact of the matter is that Nigeria and its neighbors are rooting Boko Haram out of its strongholds and degrading its combat abilities."

The new offensive comes just weeks before Nigerians holds elections many fear will be marred by violence, including from Boko Haram. The March 28 election was already postponed from Feb. 14 to enable security forces to gain control of a wide swath of northeast Nigeria where Boko Haram has roamed fairly freely, killing and kidnapping civilians with Nigeria's once-strong military becoming unable to respond. Boko Haram's leader has threatened to violently disrupt the vote and militants have warned those in the northeast not to take part.

Nigeria's President Goodluck Jonathan is running for re-election and facing great pressure to defeat a group that has killed thousands of civilians through suicide bombings targeting markets and schools. Boko Haram wants Nigeria - Africa's most populous nation - turned into a hard-line Islamic state. Jonathan has reluctantly agreed to the foreign help from Nigeria's neighbors, a humiliation for the country that already had Africa's biggest military force but whose troops are underequipped and demoralized, with corrupt officers allegedly siphoning off equipment and money.

Some analysts think the goal of stabilizing the northeast before the election will be difficult to reach.

"I don't think in six weeks they can do what they haven't been able to do in six years, but they have made advances and progress and it's that progress he (Jonathan) is very keen to show," said Adekeye Adebajo, the Nigerian executive director of the Cape Town-based Center for Conflict Resolution.

Nigerian special forces guard a compound as they participate in a hostage rescue exercise at the end of the Flintlock exercise in Mao, Chad, March 7, 2014. (AP Photo/Jerome Delay)

Boko Haram is blamed for killing at least 10,000 people in the last year alone. The violence in Nigeria has forced more than 1 million people to flee, including 100,000 to Niger, 40,000 to Cameroon and some 18,000 to Chad.

Hadisa Musa, 50, managed to escape the Boko Haram attack on the Nigerian town of Doro but only after seeing her son shot to death. She managed to spare his two children by hiding them underneath her on the ground.

Her 6-year-old grandson and 9-year-old granddaughter now stay with her in a refugee tent in Chad, after the trio spent three nights and three days in a canoe crossing Lake Chad to safety.

Her eyes moisten as she recounts their voyage, and she then pulls the fabric of her abaya up around her face, mumbling her words through the fabric.

As for the men who killed her son and scattered her family: "I don't even want to hear their name."

Boko Haram began launching attacks across the border into Cameroon earlier this year. Its fighters later struck at Niger, pounding the town of Diffa several days over the course of several days. And then on Feb. 13, jihadists in wooden boats came ashore to Chad where they torched homes and killed at least eight civilians.

When the war came to those countries, the mostly impoverished Nigerians who had fled Boko Haram violence back home were traumatized as they came under attack once again.

Chad's leader has vowed that Boko Haram and its leader Abubakar Shekau will be defeated one way or another. Chadian troops on March 2 seized the Nigerian town of Dikwa from Boko Haram, President Idriss Deby noted.

"He escaped justice during the taking of Dikwa by the Chadian army," Idriss told reporters last week. "But we know where he is. And if he refuses to surrender he will face the same fate as the others who perished in their defeat at Dikwa."

Chadian troops previously stationed by the Sudanese border make a stop on their way to Lake Chad near Baga Sola. Large contingents of Chadian troops were seen heading to the region bordering Nigeria, where residents and an intelligence officer said Boko Haram fighters are massing at their headquarters in the northeast Nigerian town of Gwoza in preparation for a showdown with multinational forces, March 6, 2015. (AP Photo / Jerome Delay)

ISIS and Boko Haram Team Up
March 13, 2015
By Christopher Torchia

It sounds chilling: two of the world's most powerful extremist movements, one in the Middle East and the other in Africa, team up to spread their harsh brand of Islamic rule.

The quick acceptance by the so-called Islamic State of Boko Haram's pledge of fealty is a publicity boost, and comes at a time when both are suffering combat losses. Boko Haram militants in Nigeria and the Islamic State group in Iraq and Syria, 2,000 miles (3,200 kilometers) away, might declare joint operations, possibly using an IS affiliate in chaotic Libya as a bridge to move arms and fighters. But whether they can effectively do that is very much in question.

What is certain is that recent developments, including the newly declared alliance, have deepened the internationalization of the almost 6-year-old Nigerian conflict.

Multinational efforts to crush the West African militants echo the disparate array of forces, including U.S. air power and Iran-backed Shiite militias, which are fighting the Islamic State group.

Already, forces from Chad, Cameroon and Niger are waging an offensive against Boko Haram. On top of that, Nigeria acknowledged late Thursday that it is getting help from regional security operatives amid reports that South African and other foreign contractors are in the fight against Boko Haram.

Chadian women walk past destroyed homes, in the Lake Chad shore village of N'Gouboua. Boko Haram militants arrived in N'gouboua before dawn on Feb. 13, marking the first attack of its kind on Chad. By the time the scorched-earth attack ended, they had burned scores of mud-brick houses by torching them with gasoline and had killed at least eight civilians and two security officers. Some 3,400 Nigerian refugees had been living in the village at the time of the attack, and all have since been relocated further inland, March 5, 2015. (AP Photo/Jerome Delay)

One South African security contractor was killed during operations earlier this week in the Maiduguri area in northeast Nigeria, where Boko Haram is active, according to South African media. Nigeria has not commented directly on the role of any South African contractors, some of whom are believed to be veterans of the apartheid-era security forces. A number of those veterans worked for the now-defunct Executive Outcomes, a private military outfit from South Africa that played a role in conflicts in Sierra Leone, Angola and other African countries in the 1990s.

France said it will slightly increase its troop numbers by the end of the year in the Sahel, which includes the Lake Chad region where most of the fighting between Boko Haram and soldiers from Nigeria and neighboring countries is taking place.

A Fulani woman and child cross a tributary of Lake Chad to the village of N'Gouboua, Chad, using the same route the Nigerian refugees used to flee Boko Haram, March 5, 2015. (AP Photo/Jerome Delay)

"We do not intend to take part in the fighting," French Defense Minister Jean-Yves Le Drian said this week. France currently has 3,000 troops involved in Operation Barkhane, a campaign against Islamic extremists in the region.

The Islamic State group was quick to accept Boko Haram's allegiance on Thursday, in contrast to slower deliberation on the pledges of other militants, some of whom abandoned al-Qaida affiliates to do so.

Boko Haram's pledge stirred fresh debate about whether Islamic State is extending its global reach. Nigerian extremists have been weakened recently by the multinational force and the Islamic State group is also under pressure from Iraqi troops and allied Shiite militias that have swept into the Iraqi city of Tikrit.

One analyst downplayed the idea of "any kind of organizational linkage" between Boko Haram and the Islamic State group.

"These movements are trying to outdo one another in terms of radicalization and scare tactics," said Jakkie Cilliers, executive director of the Institute for Security Studies, based in Pretoria, South Africa.

J. Peter Pham, director of the Africa Center at the Atlantic Council, a research center in Washington, said increasing Western assistance to the multinational African military effort against Boko Haram and the role of South African and other contractors "make this fight all that more appealing to the Islamist extremists."

"Militants finding it increasingly harder to get to Syria and Iraq may choose instead to go to northeastern Nigeria and internationalize that conflict," Pham wrote in an email to The Associated Press.

Many militants have traveled to Syria through Turkey, which has pledged tighter border controls under international pressure. On Friday, it said authorities had detained 16 Indonesians who were trying to cross the border to join the Islamic State group.

Following Boko Haram's pledge, the Nigerian government may hope for more support from the United States and other countries, said Antony Goldman, a Nigeria analyst and head of London-based firm PM Consulting. Nigerian militants, in turn, could hope for "logistics, leadership and personnel," possibly from Libyan groups, he said.

Libya, which has an Islamic State affiliate, could provide a locale for joint training and operations planning.

The purported unofficial involvement of South Africans in the conflict in support of Nigeria's government could prove problematic when they return home.

South African media have quoted South African Defense Minister Nosiviwe Mapisa-Nqakula as saying earlier this year that those South Africans were "mercenaries" and should be prosecuted when they return home.

Nigerian government spokesman Mike Omeri denied that his government is engaging in "any backchannel or unlawful recruitment." He would only say that "individuals" from the region "are on the ground in a capacity limited to training or technical support."

Islamic State Group Accepts Boko Haram
March 13, 2015
By Zeina Karam

Islamic State militants have accepted a pledge of allegiance by the Nigerian-grown Boko Haram extremist group, according to a spokesman for the Islamic State movement.

The development Thursday (March 12) came as both groups - among the most ruthless in the world - are under increasing military pressure and have sustained setbacks on the battlefield.

Nigerian troops patrol in the north-eastern Nigerian city of Mubi, some 14 miles west of the Cameroon border. Nigerian troops recaptured Mubi from Boko Haram militants in February 2015. On Friday March 13, 2015, the Islamic State group's media arm Al-Furqan, in an audio recording by spokesman Abu Mohammed al-Adnani, said that Boko Haram's pledge of allegiance has been accepted, claiming the caliphate has now expanded to West Africa, March 9, 2015. (AP Photo/str)

Islamic State seized much of northern and western Iraq last summer, gaining control of about a third of both Iraq and Syria. But it is now struggling against Iraqi forces seeking to recapture Saddam Hussein's hometown of Tikrit, while coming under fire from U.S.-led coalition air strikes in other parts of the country and in Syria.

Boko Haram, meanwhile, has been weakened by a multinational force that has dislodged it from a score of northeastern Nigerian towns. But its new

Twitter account, increasingly slick and more frequent video messages, and a new media arm all were considered signs that the group is now being helped by IS propagandists.

Then on Saturday, Boko Haram leader Abubakar Shekau posted an audio recording online that pledged allegiance to IS.

"We announce our allegiance to the Caliph of the Muslims ... and will hear and obey in times of difficulty and prosperity, in hardship and ease, and to endure being discriminated against, and not to dispute about rule with those in power, except in case of evident infidelity regarding that which there is a proof from Allah," said Boko Haram's message.

On Thursday, the Islamic State group's media arm Al-Furqan, in an audio recording by spokesman Abu Mohammed al-Adnani, said that Boko Haram's pledge of allegiance has been accepted, claiming the caliphate has now expanded to West Africa and that "no one can stand in its path."

Al-Adnani had urged foreign fighters from around the world to migrate and join Boko Haram. He also sent a message to Christians and other non-Muslims in IS lands to convert to Islam or pay a special tax - something the extremists have already put into practice in IS-held territory in Iraq and Syria.

"If you insist on being arrogant and stubborn ... soon you will bite your fingers off in regret," he added.

J. Peter Pham, director of the Africa Center at the Atlantic Council, a think tank in Washington, noted the Islamic State group's quick acceptance of Boko Haram's allegiance and said that the bond highlights a new risk.

"Militants finding it increasingly harder to get to Syria and Iraq may choose instead to go to northeastern Nigeria and internationalize that conflict," Pham wrote in an email to The Associated Press.

In the past - as was the case with IS affiliates in Egypt, Yemen and Libya - it took weeks for the Islamic State to respond to a pledge of allegiance.

"The prompt - one might even say 'fast-tracked' - acceptance by the so-called Islamic State of Boko Haram's pledge of allegiance" underscores that both needed the propaganda boost from the affiliation, Pham added.

The Boko Haram's pledge comes as the militants reportedly were massing in the northeastern Nigerian town of Gwoza, considered their headquarters, for a showdown with the Chadian-led multinational force.

Boko Haram killed an estimated 10,000 people last year, and it is blamed for last April's abduction of more than 275 schoolgirls. Thousands of Nigerians have fled to neighboring Chad.

The group is waging a nearly 6-year insurgency to impose Islamic law, or Shariah, in Nigeria. It began launching attacks across the border into Cameroon last year, and this year its fighters struck in Niger and Chad in retaliation to their agreement to form a multinational force to fight the militants.

Boko Haram followed the lead of IS in August by declaring an Islamic caliphate in northeast Nigeria that grew to cover an area the size of Belgium. After their blitz last year, Islamic State extremists declared a caliphate in the territory they control in Iraq and Syria and imposed their harsh interpretation of Islamic law.

The Nigerian group has also followed IS in publishing videos of beheadings. The latest one, published March 2, borrowed certain elements from IS productions, such as the sound of a beating heart and heavy breathing immediately before the execution, according to SITE Intelligence Group.

In video messages last year, Boko Haram's leader sent greetings and praise to both IS leader Abu Bakr al-Baghdadi and leaders of al-Qaida. The Islamic State, formerly known as the Islamic State of Iraq and the Levant, is in itself an al-Qaida breakaway that was rejected by the global terror network after the two had a brutal falling out more than a year ago.

Boko Haram, however, has never been an affiliate of al-Qaida, some analysts surmise because al-Qaida considers the Nigerians' indiscriminate slaughter of Muslim civilians as un-Islamic.

Recent offensives have marked a sharp escalation by African nations against Boko Haram. An African Union summit agreed on sending a force of 8,750 troops to fight Boko Haram.

Military operations in Niger's east have killed at least 500 Boko Haram fighters since Feb. 8, Nigerien officials have said.

Members of the U.N. Security Council proposed Thursday that the international community supply money, equipment, troops and intelligence to a five-nation African force fighting Boko Haram.

Also Thursday, Nigeria acknowledged it is getting help from regional security operatives following reports that South African and other foreign contractors are assisting in the fight against Boko Haram. Government spokesman Mike Omeri said Nigeria has extensive experience in coordinating with other African militaries and leading peacekeeping missions across the continent.

Cameroon soldiers stand guard at a lookout post as they take part in operations against the Islamic extremists group Boko Haram, their guard post is on Elbeid Bridge, left rear, that separates northern Cameroon form Nigeria's Borno state near the village of Fotokol, Cameroon. Cameroon officials say prisons are overcrowded with suspected Islamic extremists whose insurgency has spilled from Nigeria, February 25, 2015. (AP Photo/Edwin Kindzeka Moki)

Omeri noted the involvement of soldiers from regional militaries in the fight against Boko Haram, and said other "individuals" from the region "are on the ground in a capacity limited to training or technical support."

THE AP EMERGENCY RELIEF FUND

When Hurricane Katrina hit the Gulf Coast in 2005, many Associated Press staffers and their families were personally affected. AP employees rallied to help these colleagues by setting up the AP Emergency Relief Fund, which has since become a source of crucial assistance worldwide to AP staff and their families who have suffered damage or loss as a result of conflict or natural disasters.

Established as an independent 501(c)(3), the Fund provides a quick infusion of cash to help staff and their families rebuild homes, relocate and repair and replace damaged possessions.

The AP donates the net proceeds from AP Essentials, AP's company store, to the Fund.

How to Give

In order to be ready to help the moment emergencies strike, the Fund relies on the generous and ongoing support of the extended AP community. Donations can be made any time at http://www.ap.org/relieffund and are tax deductible.

On behalf of the AP staffers and families who receive aid in times of crisis, the AP Emergency Relief Fund Directors and Officers thank you.

ALSO AVAILABLE FROM AP EDITIONS

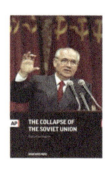

CPSIA information can be obtained at www.ICGtesting.com
Printed in the USA
LVOW02s0859220815

451135LV00019B/85/P